MASS DELUSIONS

How they harm sustainable energy, climate policy, fusion, and fusion breeding

Wallace Manheimer

Title: MASS DELUSIONS

How they harm sustainable energy, climate policy, fusion, and fusion breeding

ISBN: 979-8-88676-657-8

Author: Wallace Manheimer

Cover image: Wallace Manheimer

Publisher: Generis Publishing
Online orders: www.generis-publishing.com
Contact email: info@generis-publishing.com

Dedication

This book mentions 3 people no longer with us, David Rose, Dan Meneley, and George Stanford. They have made great contributions to the development of fusion and fission. They have certainly contributed to my understanding and education, and I thank them for it. This book is dedicated to their memory. May future users of fission and fusion remember these contributions to their lifestyles and prosperity. I also dedicate it to my wife Eileen, my children Karen, Eric and Howard, and my grandchildren, Isaac, Zachary, Clara and Isabella. May these people, especially my grandchildren mature, prosper, and contribute to a world where power is a given, not one where it is taken away by mass delusions.

Contents

Prologue...9

I. Sustainable energy from the top down. 21

II. While Climate has changed and always will, the is no climate crisis..................37

    The Climate Industrial Complex 37

    The Chicken Littles of the Climate Industrial Complex...................................42

    Some naked emperors of the climate industrial complex, and others 46

    A brief tour of CO_2 induced radiation forcing in the atmosphere 55

    Climate change over the period of human civilization....................................62

    Climate over a geological time scale...67

    What an internet search says about climate change 69

III. Some problems with wind and solar power 75

    The solar and wind power available..77

    The (un)reliability of solar power..80

    The material requirements for solar and wind..88

    The cost for delivered power...89

    The end of the life cycle 92

    Subsidies and total cost for the transition to decarbonize 99

IV. Fusion 106

    The fusion reactions...106

    Magnetic fusion, The triple fusion product 110

    The tokamak program...113

    L, H and super H modes of tokamak operation..120

    ITER's pure fusion's scientific dilemma 123

    Conservative design rules..124

    Fusion start-ups' pilot plants all have serious problems and will most likely fail 138

    Inertial Fusion..148

V. Fusion breeding 169

    Why fusion breeding?..169

    What is fusion breeding 170

    Preliminary development plans for achieving fusion breeding by mid century.................184

What if a viable pure fusion device suddenly becomes available? 197

The energy park 199

Epilogue 205

DISCLAIMER 209

Prologue

The of the title of this monograph is taken from a rather well-known quote by Richard Lindzen, a climate change skeptic, and probably the world's greatest authority on geophysical fluid motions:

"What historians will definitely wonder about in future centuries is how deeply flawed logic, obscured by shrewd and unrelenting propaganda, actually enabled a coalition of powerful special interests to convince nearly everyone in the world that CO_2 from human industry was a dangerous, planet-destroying toxin. It will be remembered as the greatest mass delusion in the history of the world- that CO_2, the life of plants, was considered for a time to be a deadly poison."

Unfortunately, mass delusions are a part of life, in the United States and in the rest of the world, today and throughout history. Once they have ended, it is not easy to understand why they ever occurred, but when the masses are in their grip, they can hardly be challenged. This author has written about three such mass delusions in American history, the Salem witchcraft trials in 1692, the McCarthy communist witch hunts 1950-54, and the persecution of preschool teachers for assumed preschool sex abuse in the 1980's and 90's. He makes the case that the fixation on an onrushing climate catastrophe is another:

Wallace Manheimer, Original sin, prophets, witches, communists, preschool sex abuse, and climate change

International Journal of Engineering and Applied Sciences (IJEAS) ISSN: 2394-3661, Volume-4, Issue-7, July 2017

https://www.ijeas.org/download_data/IJEAS0407025.pdf

One very discouraging thing about these mass delusions, is that as communications got easier, better, and faster, one might think that society would come to its senses more and more quickly as time progressed. Instead, the opposite has happened. Salem came to its senses in less than a year. The McCarthy terror lasted 4 years, and the preschool sex abuse lasted nearly 20. In each case, one hero, let's call her or him a 'good witch', was largely responsible for ending the mass delusion. In Salem, it was Governor Phipps, who ended the use of 'specular evidence'. In the Mc Carthy witch hunt it was Joseph Welsh, the Army's counsel, who exposed Senator McCarthy's needless cruelty. In the preschool sex abuse case, it was Dorothy Rabinowitz, who over the decades, tirelessly wrote columns in the Wall Street Journal exposing the madness of it. The climate catastrophe mass delusion has been going on for 30 years now with no end in sight, its claws have been reaching into the highest levels of western government, business, media, and scientific societies. So far no 'good witch' has succeeded in turning things around, although there have been many applicants for the job, certainly including Richard Lindzen, likely many other scientists to be mentioned here, and perhaps even this author.

This monograph is principally about energy, which is essential for modern civilization. However, most of the world does not have sufficient energy. Bringing the entire human family up to OECD standards is difficult but is vital. This manuscript sets out the goal of doing so by mid-century. In the Jewish religion, we would call it tikum olam, or repairing the world.

However, the manuscript is not only about energy; it is also about how false information about a scientific subject can guide a society into disastrously wrong directions and argues for what it sees as more productive directions. Furthermore, it must deal with another related subject besides energy. After all, if you want to learn about traffic on the freeway, sometimes you have to look at the side roads too. That is very much the situation with energy and the fear of a climate crisis. This author has published information on this in bits and pieces. Some publishers and scientific organizations refused to touch any of it (mass delusion?), other would publish this but not that, or that but not this.... Hence, when the publisher of this volume, seeing some of my open access publications, solicited me to put it all together in a single monograph, well, what happens when you offer an alcoholic a drink? This is a unified matter, and it is presented best in a single volume of this size when all aspects are considered.

Hence large parts of the book are taken from various open access papers the author has published. Many of the images in both the papers listed below, and in this manuscript have been taken directly off the internet.

Regarding images taken from scientific papers, the publishers of the 4 first papers listed below, papers in major American or British journals, only requested that any copyrighted material be properly referenced, and of course it was. At no point did the editors request that I ask for explicit permissions from the original user.

Hence, this author then owns the copyright of all those open access publications, as well as the 3 below, and anyone has permission to use them any way he or she wishes, as long as the user cites the appropriate publication, which of course I do right here.

Four of these open access publications are mostly about fusion breeding, and they are published in what anyone would call first rate, rigorously reviewed journals. These are:

Fusion breeding for mid-century, sustainable, carbon free power
WallaceManheimer, Heliyon (Cell Press) Volume 6, Issue 9, September 2020, Fusion breeding for mid-century, sustainable, carbon free power

Midcentury carbon free sustainable energy development based on fusion breeding, Wallace Manheimer, IEEE Access, December 2018, Vol 6, issue 1, p 64954-64969, https://ieeexplore.ieee.org/document/8502757

Fusion Breeding for Midcentury Sustainable Power, Wallace Manheimer
Journal of Fusion Energy June 2014 (open access) vol 33, p 199
https://link.springer.com/article/10.1007/s10894-014-9690-9

and

Manheimer, W. Fusion breeding as an approach to sustainable energy. *Discover Sustainability* **1,** 4 (2020).

https://doi.org/10.1007/s43621-020-00004-9

The work on climate change and windmills was much more difficult to publish in American journals of the quality of those above. This author has attempted to do so on several occasions and has met only with immediate rejection, or one might say, rejection as the envelope was being opened, that is immediate rejection by the editor (or whoever 'opened the envelop') without even bothering sending it to reviewers. Accordingly, this work was published in a Canadian journal: "The Canadian Center of Science and Education (CCSE) is a private for-profit organization delivering support and services to educators and researchers in Canada and around the world (from the CCSE web site)". I believe it is a very high-quality journal and publishing enterprise. These open access publications are:

Wallace Manheimer, Civilization Needs Sustainable Energy – Fusion Breeding May Be Best, Journal of Sustainable Development, Volume 15, page 98, 2022

https://ccsenet.org/journal/index.php/jsd/article/view/0/46729

This not only spoke of fusion breeding, but also of the inability of windmills and solar panels to provide relevant power, seemingly making it unpublishable in standard American Journals.

Wallace Manheimer, While the climate always has, and always will change, There is no climate crisis, Vol. 15, No. 5, p. 116 (2022), Journal of Sustainable Development

https://ccsenet.org/journal/index.php/jsd/article/view/0/47745

The author does not use social media, however somebody else attempted to distribute the latter of these on Facebook. To illustrate the difficulty of scientific communication regarding the climate dilemma, this work was fact checked and cancelled by Facebook. *The paper was controversial, but the science in it is solid and correct; it should not have been cancelled.* Mass delusion at work? Without mentioning any names, this author is familiar with a few of these 'fact checkers'. Hopefully without appearing overly immodest, they do not have nearly my scientific qualifications, and most certainly do not have even a tiny fraction of the qualifications of many other outstanding scientists mentioned in this work.

Speaking of canceling work, the author wrote another manuscript on fusion breeding, this one solicited by the journal Fusion Science and Technology (FST), (published by the American Nuclear Society) for its special issue on wide ranging and exotic uses of fusion technology. My manuscript argued that 1. The 'fusion start ups', namely private companies promising commercial fusion in ~ a decade, will all fail, and argued that using a false climate crisis to fund their projects is a serious error, 2. It analyzed ways fusion breeding can come to commercial use. It was accepted with high marks by the reviewers and editor, but despite this, after several months the journal publisher cancelled it. Possibly mass delusion at work again. I archived it right away as:

Wallace Manheimer , Fusion breeding and pure fusion development – perceptions and misperceptions http://arxiv.org/abs/2212.00907 Dec 5, 2022

However, I also wanted a regular publication and especially one that could be rapid. I did not want to resubmit it to an American journal. For one thing, at very best, it meant a delay of at least quite a few months. Much more likely it would suffer the same fate. Hence, I looked around for one of the many journals that solicit my input. I liked the idea of an Indian journal, as India is now a full-fledged member of the ITER collaboration. I decided on:

Wallace Manheimer, Fusion breeding and pure fusion development perceptions and misperceptions, International Journal of Engineering, Applied Science and Technology, 2022, Volume 7, https://www.ijeast.com/current-issue.php , p 125-154

Furthermore, this paper added an Appendix describing fully the experience with FST, the positive reviews by both the reviewers and editors, and finally after months of being incommunicado to my requests for information on publishing, sent me a brusque letter rejection it for reasons which were obviously false. Likely they did not want to publish a paper which, as the second reviewer of the manuscript, pointed out, "cast doubt on the religion of climate change".

There are 5 parts to this monograph. The first is about energy, how much we have, how much we need, and the ways of getting there. It concludes that if we want civilization to survive for the entire human family, in the long run, we must turn to nuclear energy. But what sort of nuclear energy? This is not that much ^{235}U available from mines. Ultimately, we must turn to breeding. Breeding is a seemingly magical way of producing fuel for thermal nuclear reactors. It takes an element which appears in nature like thorium and bombards it with neutrons and ends up with a perfectly good fuel for thermal reactors, ^{233}U in this case. Modern alchemy at work! Again, producing something essential from scarcity is something that religious traditions have dreamt of for millennia. The Jewish religion has its Hanukkah celebration of the victory over the Syrians 2000 years ago. To rededicate the temple, they had only one jar of sacramental oil, however it burned for 8 days. In Christianity, there is of course the parable of Jesus feeding the masses with five loaves of bread and two fish. In other words, these two examples emphasize the intense desire of mankind, over the millenia, to provide abundance from scarcity. This is something fusion breeding might well be able to do. But to get back to breeding, there are a variety of ways to breed both via fission and via fusion. This section very briefly introduces the idea of fusion breeding. The physics in this section is simple. There is no reason a bright, motivated high school student who has had a physics course cannot follow virtually all of it.

Second, there is the climate dilemma. Somehow the false idea that we are on the cusp of a climate crisis, caused by burning fossil fuel, which adds CO_2 to the atmosphere, has taken hold, at least in the western world. Numerous UN documents say that the world temperature increase must be kept below $1.5^{\circ}C$ above the preindustrial value, or catastrophe will result. But the temperature has already increased more than $1^{\circ}C$ above the preindustrial value. We may not be at the catastrophe level yet, but we are *pretty close*; things *should* certainly be *pretty bad* now. Yet by every measure, related to environment and individuals, things are much better than they were in 1910 when the temperature was a degree lower. Surely, this argues for extreme skepticism that another less than half degree will produce catastrophe.

Believers claim that there is a strong scientific consensus to this fiction. (I use here the less confrontational terms 'believers' and 'skeptics', rather than the often used and pejorative terms: 'alarmists' and 'deniers'.) But as we will see, there are at least tens of thousands of highly qualified scientists denying this claim (www.petitionproject.org;   https://clintel.org/world-climate-declaration). Believers argue, "yes, but they are not climate scientists!". Well, what is a climate scientist? Richard Lindzen is just about the world's leading authority on geophysical fluid dynamics. Is he not a 'climate scientist'? William Happer is about the world's leading authority on the interaction of radiation with complex molecules, the very basis of the greenhouse effect. Is he not a 'climate scientist'? Judith Curry, was the former head of earth science at Georgia Tech, but left the academic world due to its stultifying demands for conformity. Is she not a 'climate scientist'? What about Steven Koonin, one of the world leading physicists, who made discoveries in many areas of physics and recently wrote a book called Unsettled (presumably to mock the claim that regarding climate 'the science is settled') disputing the current climate emergency dogma. Is he not a climate scientist? What about Bjorn Lomborg (Time Magazine counts him as one of the 100 most influential people in the world), Patrick Moore and Michael Shellenberg, three of the world's leading environmentalists, each of whom has written a book denying the climate crisis. Are they not 'climate scientists? Actually, nobody is a 'climate scientist', the science relating to climate is so vast, including just about every field of science and engineering, that nobody can master even a tiny fraction of it. Aspects of the detailed physics of climate change can be complex but testing the claims and predictions of the believers is simple. Doing so, one sees that there is neither a climate crisis now nor on the visible horizon.

Third there is the issue of wind and solar power with battery backups. Believers argue that these 'clean, reliable, and sustainable' energy sources are just about ready to replace coal, oil, and natural gas, if they cannot do so already. It is even argued that they are cheaper. However, these claims are all false, especially the claim that they are 'clean'. In fact when all is taken into account, they are by far the dirtiest power sources, as this book will show. In this case, the physics involved very simple. As in the first section, there is no reason a motivated, bright high school senior who has taken a high school physics course, cannot follow just about all of Section 3 of this book.

Fourth there is controlled fusion, and unfortunately the physics here is *not* simple. This section simplifies the physics as much as possible while not overdoing it.

The author has spent about half of his more than 50-year career as a scientist at the Naval Research Laboratory in Washington DC doing research on controlled fusion. (The other half was on a variety of problems related to national defense.) Very briefly controlled fusion is the attempt to control the reaction that drives the hydrogen bomb. This requires a very hot dense state of matter which is somehow confined, either by its own inertia (as in the bomb) or by some other means. In the laboratory, the attempt is made to do something similar by compressing the target with a powerful laser; or else confining the ionized reacting gases (called plasmas) in a high magnetic field. Neither is easy, and the fusion project has been under active research for well over 60 years. The question is will it ever succeed? At the outset of the project, the claim was that we would have economical fusion in ~ 35 years. Now, 60 years later, that time estimate is still 35 more years. However, the false climate crisis has caused several companies to claim that they now have a way to produce economical fusion on a much shorter time scale, a decade, or maybe even less. We will show that these assertions simply cannot be true.

The fifth section is on fusion breeding, a variation on fusion which may well be attainable in the often mentioned 35 years. For more than 20 years, this author has argued for, and researched this other option, namely using fusion neutrons to breed fuel for thermal nuclear reactors. This makes the requirement on the fusion confinement system about *an order of magnitude easier to achieve*! Fuel for thermal reactors may be in short supply not too long after mid-century, especially if the remainder of the world develops as this manuscript hopes and argues for. There is also the possibility of breeding via the straight fast neutron nuclear route, but if fusion breeding could be achieved, it would have many advantages over fission breeding. A single fusion breeder could fuel 5-10 thermal nuclear reactors of equal power; it would take two fission breeders at maximum breeding rate to fuel one. With fusion breeding, the 35-year time scale for economical fusion could finally be realized, not only in our dreams, but also in reality.

However, fusion breeding has been the ugly duckling of the fusion project, rejected by most, but certainly not all of the fission and fusion community. But it should no longer be ignored, nor ignorantly condemned with such erroneous remarks as: "it combines the worst aspects of fusion with the worst aspects of fission", or "fusion breeding can only address fuel, the one problem that fission does NOT have". This paper, and others, hope turn fusion breeding into the beautiful swan.

I will continue with some remarks about the American Physical Society (APS). I am a life fellow, and this is the professional society with which I most closely associate. (I am also a life fellow of the Institute of Electrical and Electronic Engineers [IEEE]). Unfortunately, the APS is very much under control of strict believers in the standard climate dogma, and strict believers in only conventional fusion. At least in my own experience, they are unwilling to consider any heretical views. I have submitted at least half a dozen manuscripts to various APS and AIP (American Institute of Physics) journals on these topics, and all have been immediately rejected by the editor; seemingly as they opened the envelop; they never even went to a reviewer. Fortunately (for me), other organizations and publishers at least as prestigious and with as much gravitas as APS especially IEEE have accepted my work; and so have publishers with as much reputation and gravitas as APS (IEEE, Springer and the Cell network). Also, the afore mentioned CCSE, has been willing to publish my work with proper reviewing. However, there is one small element of the APS that is willing to consider heretical viewpoints, and that is the Forum on Physics and Society. They publish a quarterly pamphlet on a variety of subjects on the interaction of physics and society. I have used it to discuss both climate and fusion breeding issues. For this I have to compliment the two editors I have worked with, Cameron Reed and Oriol Valls. The author hopes that this monograph, will in some small way, help to convince the APS to loosen its restrictions, follow the examples of the two editors I just mentioned, and to realize that the articles of faith, which it sees as having descended from the mountain, just might not be correct.

Concluding are 6 questions, which the believers and pure fusion advocates should answer, and yet they have not yet done so:

1. Carbon dioxide is necessary for life on this planet in just the same way that oxygen is. CO_2 is necessary for plants, oxygen for animals (obviously including humans). Without CO_2, there could be no plants, and without plants, there could be no animals. Hence what do the believers think is the optimum level of atmospheric CO_2 ¬and why?

2. It is very easy to use the internet to find articles asserting that windmills and solar panels are now, or will soon be cheaper than coal, gas or nuclear. If this is true, why is power so much more expensive and so much less reliable in places that rely to a large extent on wind and solar?

3. To avoid a climate catastrophe, it is often said that it is imperative to keep the world temperature increase to a level of 1.5oC below the preindustrial value. But the temperature has already risen by at least 1oC and there is not even the slightest sign of any catastrophe.

4. It is believers and proponents who claim a very large cost to transition to carbon free energy. See Vaclav Smil, IEEE Spectrum, October 2022, which gives a conservative estimate of the cost at $275T between 2021 and 2050. Are the better things the world could spend $275T on? This author considers it to be a near total waste of enormous resources which could be used in much better ways. Resource wastes of that magnitude have a real possibility of destroying modern civilization.

5. Pure fusion has been predicting economic fusion power in ~35 years for more than 60 years now. Many private 'fusion start ups' have recently predicted it can be done in 10, citing the almost certain false fear of an imminent climate disaster. Where is the new experimental data that shows now that it can be done in ~10? There have been hardly any new advances on experiments on large tokamaks in in the last 10-20 years.

6. Why has fusion breeding been constantly denigrated, when it clearly reduces the requirements of the fusion device by at least an order of magnitude? Or as Patrick Moore wrote in an email to me in 2022: "Why has your pathway not been pursued, especially when the direct fusion approach has never produced what's needed?"

I. Sustainable energy from the top down.

Modern civilization needs energy. Before fossil fuel became widely used, this energy was provided by people and animals. Because this constituted so little energy, civilization had been a thin veneer atop a vast mountain of human squalor and misery, a veneer maintained by such institutions as slavery, colonialism and tyranny. Fossil fuel has extended the benefits of modern civilization to billions, but its job, in this respect is not yet complete. There are still billions on earth who derive little benefit from this power source, and billions more who derive hardly any. To spread the benefits of modern civilization to the entire human family would require much more energy, as well as newer sources of energy.

Thirty years ago, one could envision civilization advancing by the spread of fossil fuel, to be gradually replaced by nuclear energy, to be fueled at first by mined uranium, and then by breeding fissile material, either by nuclear fission or nuclear fusion; and possibly even fusion itself. Even now, this is the proper way of achieving sustainable energy which is economically and environmentally viable.

However thirty years ago, a gigantic monkey wrench was thrown into this vision. This is the fear that the continued burning of fossil fuel would put too much CO_2 into the earth's atmosphere and cause possibly catastrophic climate change in a short time, a decade or two. Based on this fear, the the western world is in the process of switching its power source to wind and solar, with battery backups for times when there is no wind or solar. As we discuss, the bitter experience of those countries (England and Germany) and regions (Texas and California) that have implemented these on a large scale have shown it to be unreliable, very expensive, and environmentally disastrous, both locally and in the areas where they mine the material for it, and in the areas where they dispose of its trash. Helen Raleigh even compared the rush toward solar and wind to be comparable to the

Great Leap Forward, the disastrous China policy of rapid forced industrialization which caused only poverty, squalor and starvation in China for years (1). She called it "The Green Leap Forward.

Furthermore, it is easy to flip a switch and the light goes on, right? Well, ask the people who work in the power plant, or the people who work in the coal mines, or the people who string up the power lines how easy it is. This must be kept in mind when we are talking about changing our energy infrastructure for whatever reason.

The assumption that electricity is 'easy', can lead one to underestimate the difficulties. For instance, there is currently a push to electrify auto transport in the United States with such cars as the Tesla. President Biden has repeatedly advocated that America spend the money for 500,000 charging stations so these cars can recharge virtually anywhere. But what will they recharge with? Will there be enough electrical power to do so?

American autos and trucks today use ~ 340 million gallons of gasoline per day. The energy equivalent of a gallon of gas i.e. ~ 40 kWhrs, so they use about 14 Billion kWhrs per day, or dividing by the 24 hours in a day, about 600 GW. However electric motors are about three times as efficient as Gasoline motors, so electric cars will use about 200 GW of electric power.

America now generates ~ 400GW of electrical power. In other words, to electrify ground transportation in America, the country would have to increase its generating capacity very quickly by ~ 50%, where it took generations to build up the current American electrical infrastructure. No problem, it is 'easy'.

One excellent source of these statistics is the yearly publications by BP (2). Taken from their 2019 issue are their graphs of the sources of energy, the energy use in various parts of the world, and by end use.

Prmary energy demand
Billion toe

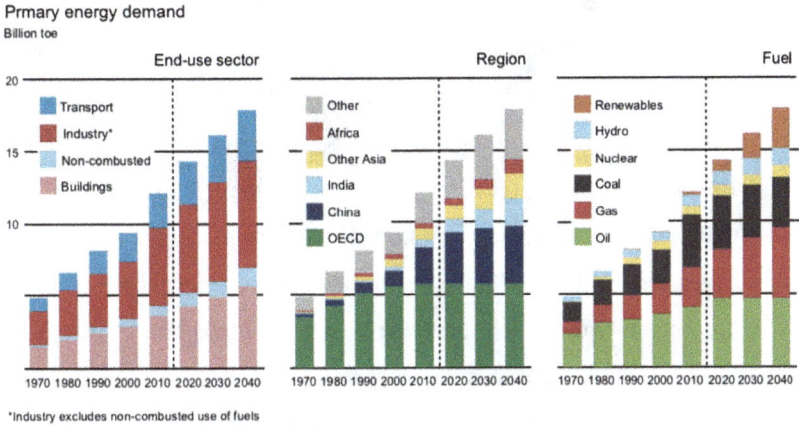

Figure (1): BP's three graphs of energy demand by end use sector, region and fuel. The units are billions of tons of oil per year. Since this is an unusual unit for people not in the oil industry, we use terawatts (TW), where one terawatt is approximately one billion tons of oil per year. Taken from Ref (2)

To the left of their vertical dashed line in Fig. (1) is the historical record. To the right are BP's extrapolations for the future. While up to 2040 BP sees fossil fuel as playing a very important role, it is not sustainable. That is it will run out at some point.

Plagiarizing a bit from the Declaration of Independence, the author holds this truth to be self-evident, namely that it must be the goal of the world to bring the entire world up to OECD standards, soon, say by mid-century. As is apparent from the graph, the world today uses about 14 terawatts (TW). However the energy use is very unequal. The 1.2 billion people in the economically more advanced OECD countries use ~ 6 TW, or ~ 5 kilowatt (kW) per capita. The other 7 billion or so people living on the planet share 8 TW, or use ~ 1 kW per capita. The world's goal certainly must be to bring the rest of the world up to OECD standards of

23

living as quickly as possible. By mid century the world population is expected to level off at about 10B, meaning that at current OECD power use, the world would need as much as 50TW!

The developing world will use whatever fuel works best, and very likely at this time, that is coal. The Chinese and Indians are very rapidly and enormously increasing their coal use today. China today is by far the largest CO_2 emitter in the world, and they are still building coal fired power plants at a rapid pace. India is doing everything it can to catch up. Soon Africa, the rest of Asia, and Latin America will do the same. Nothing can stop this. In fact, modern coal fired power plants are very clean. The United States has developed a new coal power plant called Ultra Super Critical. It burns at a higher temperature, meaning its efficiency is now ~40% rather than the more traditional 33%. Also, it is clean, in that the only effluents are CO_2 and water vapor. All other pollutants are scrubbed out of the plant discharge. Coal could now be clean. The first ultra-super critical plant is the John Turk plant in Arkansas (3). Many more have since been built.

Coal, for next several decades, could be the salvation of, for instance, more than half of sub-Saharan Africans — the number who labor daily with inadequate supplies of electricity. The World Health Organization estimates that ~ 2.4 Billion people worldwide do their cooking, heating and lighting with a combination of wood, charcoal and dried animal dung (4). The problem is especially acute in Sub-Saharan Africa, where it estimates that about half a million die each year from the results of this indoor air pollution. Don't African lives matter?

The U.S. could, and should, be selling Africans modern supercritical plants — and working with them to set up their own plants — except for ridiculous American prohibitions due to the anti-coal mass delusion. These could be a solution to both their indoor and outdoor air pollution. Instead, they will be getting much dirtier technology from China and others. There is no stopping Africans and others from installing and building large numbers of coal plants, just as India and China are now doing. And who are we in the western world to lecture not only the Africans, but others in less developed parts of the world, to stop their march to prosperity in the way they see as most advantageous. This is especially true if this involves the use of nearly pollution free ultra-super critical coal plants.

As I hope this makes clear, the western insistence on windmills and solar power exclusively, will not only do great harm to itself ultimately, but will do much greater harm, much faster, to places like Africa, Latin America, Indonesia…. The harm that these unscientific, uneconomic, and environmentally disastrous policies are attemping to inflict on the world, and especially the less developed world should weigh heavily on the western consciences.

Also energy efficiency is also expected to increase, and typically increases by ~ ½ - 1% per year (5). Hence let us think in terms of 35-40 TW by mid century. Two ways the energy efficiency could increase are to switch from conventional coal powered generators at ~33% efficiency, to more efficient ultra super critical coal powered generators at ~ 40%. Furthermore, a portion of electricity generation could shift to gas powered generators, which typically run at ~ 50% efficiency. Undoubtedly there are many other approaches to increasing efficiency, including having more business meetings on line instead of in person.

The BP extrapolation up to 2040 is a perfect example of extrapolation 'from the bottom up'. They take what is being done now, and and see how much they can push it to advance. They see a power increase of up to ~ 2 TW per decade by 2040, or an increase of ~ 200 GW per year. Extrapolating their graph to 2050, they would probably predict a world wide power of ~20TW. However this is not nearly sufficient to bring the world up to OECD standards by then.

This author prefers interpolation 'from the top down'. That is, let's see how much power we need to get the world up to OECD standard at some particular time, which we take as mid century, 2050. This means increasing the power by ~ 21 - 25 TW by then, or ~ 7-8 TW per decade; more than triple the advance that BP foresees. This should be the goal the world strives toward. This, not climate change, is the true challenge the world must face.

Whether the concern is exhausting fossil fuel (we can use it for quite a while, but will exhaust it in 1/3 the time at 35TW as at 12), or is knowing that solar and wind cannot do the job (see section III) or knowing that pure fusion cannot do the job, at least in this century if ever (see Sections IV and V) these lead to one and only one conclusion. Nuclear power must play an important role, both in any final sustainable role, and on the way there. Let us think of a sustainable future for all mankind as one that increases nuclear power by about a factor of 20 to ~ 20TW (i.e. ~7TWe) worldwide by midcentury, reducing fossil fuel somewhat to ~10TW, so it will last at least as long as current estimates, and increasing hydro and possibly even renewables to 1-3 TW each. In other words, it still recognizes that fossil fuel will play an essential role, but less crucial than today. It does not regard the use of fossil fuel, at 10 TW well into the future, as causing an extreme planetary calamity (6). Ultimately, as fossil fuel runs out, nuclear power would take over completely, but would be quite far in the future.

This then would obviously require something of a crash program in expanding nuclear power over the next few decades. There is every reason to think this possible technically, although perhaps not politically. At least in the United States, regulations, lawsuits, protest marches, bureaucratic delays, environmental impact statements done and redone numerous times, NIMBY, BANANA,… have all thrown sand in the gears of nuclear power. These could be the biggest problem it faces. Even if the nuclear company is successful, typically 20 years are wasted as it strangles in bureaucratic red tape and court cases, enormously increasing the price of nuclear power. *Time is money*! Regulation reform is the American, and perhaps the worldwide nuclear industry's biggest battle right now.

Let us briefly now digress to discuss nuclear safety. In the light of the Fukushima nuclear disaster, the safety of nuclear reactors in the event of extreme events obviously has to be reexamined. This author has neither expertise nor suggestions but is confident this can be accomplished. However, there are a few factors worth considering regarding technology, biology, and psychology.

First consider the technology. In a nuclear disaster the main danger is to land, not people. The Fukushima earthquake and tsunami killed about 20,000 people. Hopefully, without tempting fate, the number killed so far by radiation, is zero. The people had time to get away and the nuclear workers there seem to be adequately protected. Even in Chernobyl, with a very risky reactor design no country in the west uses, and total irresponsibility of the Communist bosses of the plant (see the Netflix mini-series "Chernobyl'), where the initial prediction was many thousands of deaths, the official number is now 31 (7).

However, a large area of land near the reactors may be contaminated. Thus, after immediately getting unprotected people out of harm's way and securing the reactor, the ultimate decontamination of the land is the highest priority in a nuclear disaster. Our recommendation is that the nuclear industry dedicate considerable resources to researching what is required here and preparing (hopefully on a worldwide basis) for such an eventuality. This will be needed only very, very rarely (and hopefully never), but once needed, the need will be acute.

Now consider the biology and ask just how decontaminated the land must be for humans to safely live and work there. Humans do live in a constant bath of radiation, coming from both the sky and earth. An important issue is just how harmful is low level radiation to humans? One answer is from the cancer rates of the Hiroshima and Nagasaki survivors. In about 2010 there were roughly100,000 of them, and their health has been monitored for decades by both the American and Japanese governments. Obviously, they had been exposed to vast quantities of radiation. Yet only about 800 cases of additional cancers had been caused by this exposure [8]. In other words, fewer than 1 % of the survivors had developed a cancer which can be attributed to the radiation they received. This corresponds to about a 10 % increase in the cancer rate among the survivors. But in the United States, the state-to-state variation of cancer rate varies from about 380–510 cancers per hundred thousand people per year, an increase of 30 % from the state with the least cancer to that with the most.

While obviously nobody thinks that Hiroshima levels of radiation are acceptable, it does cause one to question just how harmful low levels are. At a level just a few times above background, the epidemiological measure of increase in cancer rate would be difficult to detect, because the natural and other man-made causes are so much higher. This assumes the linear no threshold (LNT) model; that is every little bit of radiation causes some additional increase to the cancer rate, which is proportional to the radiation increase. However, medical personnel are more and more skeptical of LNT, since cells have repair mechanisms for damaged DNA. A study by Dr. Tubiana [9] and his team, published in the US National Institute of Health journal Radiology makes the case that below some specified level, increases in radiation have no adverse effects on humans. There is even a subculture, which believe that increases in low levels of radiation are beneficial to humans (10), but this is obviously very speculative.

In any case, in decontamination of the land, technology most likely says that the levels cannot be brought to zero, and biology says they do not have to be. Likely it can be a few times above background and the result will be, at worst a nearly unmeasurable uptick in cancer rate, and more likely no increase at all.

But then there is psychology. It would be wonderful if there were an abundant, universally accepted, perfectly safe energy source. But we do not live in a perfect world. Any energy source has risks. Coal has killed many more people and destroyed much more land than nuclear ever will. Yet people seem willing to accept coal over nuclear. Any time an anti-nuclear activist lights up a cigarette, she incurs a much greater cancer risk, than she does standing outside the nuclear power plant with her sign. Driving to the demonstration, he is at much greater risk in his car. Yet these risks are all acceptable.

Who can figure? certainly not the author, who is neither a psychologist nor pastoral counselor. But these attitudes are not necessarily permanent. They can change over a generation or so, especially if the Japanese, hopefully with international help, can render the damaged reactors inert, and decontaminate and repopulate the land.

It may be that nuclear power is making a comeback. John Kerry, the man most responsible for killing the American breeder program in 1994 is now saying "Go for it" regarding a renewed American nuclear program (11). Prime minister Boris Johnson, before his resignation (i.e. in May 2022) said the UK will build one new nuclear plant a year (12). Also, it is planning an advanced breeder (an upgrade to the American Integral Fast Reactor, IFR) called the PRISM to treat its plutonium wastes (13). In February 2022 France announce plans to build at least 6 new reactors, and perhaps even an additional 8 (14).

Yet even if the nuclear industry solves its image problem, it faces a much bigger problem on the physics and technical side. Fissile ^{235}U comprises only 0.7% of the uranium resource. Supplies of mined 235U are limited, almost certainly much less than the reserve of fossil fuel. One rather pessimistic estimate is that the energy resource of mined uranium is about 60-300 Terawatt years (15).

Other estimates are higher (16), but no estimate is high enough, that if it were correct, there would be enough uranium to sustainably supply the world's thermal nuclear reactors with 20-30TW (i.e. ~6-10TWe).

Before considering breeding, let us briefly examine two other approaches for acquiring fissile fuel. First there is uranium from the oceans (15), and second there is accelerator production of uranium.

Many uranium chemicals are water soluble, and accordingly, the world's oceans have a large amount of uranium dissolved in them. In a cubic meter of sea water there is about 3.2×10^{-6} kg of uranium, for a concentration of about 3.2×10^{-9}, well below the concentration for which normal mining is economical. This translated to 1.8 MJ of nuclear fuel per m^3. There are two ways one might consider extracting it, mining it from a ship, and putting stationary nets of one type or another in ocean currents, nets which can trap the uranium chemicals. It is easy to see that mining from a ship can never work. Let's say that to get the water onto the ship, it raises the cubic meter of water (1 metric ton) 30 meters with a 30% efficient pump. This alone uses 1 MJ of the 1.8 MJ available from the sea water

Consider now trapping the uranium from an ocean current. The flow of the ^{235}U in all the world's rivers is about 2 TW [15]. Even with a series of filters which extract 100% of the uranium in the river flows, it would not be enough to extract 10 TW of fissile fuel. As Ref [15] quotes: "Getting 10 TW of primary power from ^{235}U crustal ores or seawater extraction may not be impossible, but it would be a big stretch".

The Japanese, using one of their local ocean currents have extracted uranium this way. In numerous trials, the Japanese program extracted around 100 grams per month [17] (i.e. ~ 1 gram of ^{235}U per month, or ~ 10 grams per year). Hence the extraction rate would have to increase by ~ 5 orders of magnitude to fuel a 1 GWE reactor, which burns ~ one metric ton of ^{235}U per year. It would have to increase uranium production by 8 orders to fuel 1 TW, and by 9, to fuel 10 TW. Obviously, uranium from sea water has to clear many, many hurdles.

Regarding accelerator production, a 1 GeV proton impinging on a high Z target, for instance Pb, can generate as many as 30 spallation neutrons. These can breed ^{233}U from thorium as will be described here.

But let us look at the entire process. Start with 6 GeV of chemical energy in say coal. This produces electricity with typically 1/3 efficiency, so it produces 2 GeV of wall plug electric energy, which could power the accelerator. But accelerators like this are typically 50% efficient, so it produces the 1 GeV proton. This then generates 30 spallation neutrons. Say each one produces a ^{233}U with no wasted neutrons, so we have 30 ^{233}U nuclei. If each one splits and gives 200 MeV fission fragments, the 30 nuclei will give a total energy of 6 GeV, just the energy we started with in the coal.

The accelerator production of fissile material does not give any extra energy. Perhaps it would be able to produce enough fissile material to start a fission breeder if there were no other fissile material, but it does not produce energy, it transforms chemical to nuclear energy, but adds no energy.

Ultimately breeding fuel must play an important role. Breeding means taking a material which exists in nature like, ^{238}U or ^{232}Th, called fertile materials, and bombarding them with neutrons to make fissile materials, like ^{239}Pu or ^{233}U, which do not exist in nature. However, because these have an odd atomic weight, they are fine as fuel for thermal fission reactors such a light water reactor (LWR). There are certainly conventional approaches to breeding, including fast neutron reactors (18-21), and thermal thorium reactors (22), and these certainly have a shorter development path than fusion breeding. Other countries, especially Russia and India are taking these reactors very seriously. Russia already has two fast neutron reactors, their BN 600 and BN 800 attached to their grid. (The Russian word for fast is bistro.)

Not only is the reaction cross section much greater for a thermal neutron reactor, but the thermal reactor designer has a wide choice of coolants (e.g. water or air), instead of only liquid sodium or lead, which must be used in a fast neutron reactor. Figure (2) is a plot of the fission and neutron absorption cross sections as a function of neutron energy for ^{235}U and ^{238}U (23).

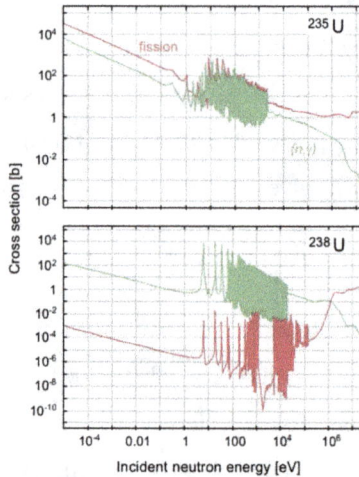

Figure 2 : The fission and neutron absorption cross section in barns (1 barn is 10^{-24} cm) for ^{235}U and ^{238}U as a function of the energy of the incident neutron. The cross sections look about the same for all fertile and fissile nuclei, depending whether their atomic number is odd or even. The red curves are the fission cross sections, and the green, are the neutron absorption cross sections. From (23)

Fission breeders, of course can, and have been developed. France also had its Super Pheenex breeder hooked up to its grid for a while until the greens' constant protests succeeded in having it decommissioned. It finally worked, but it took years to iron out all the bugs, principally difficulties with dealing with liquid sodium in the quantity necessary to cool the reactor (18). The United States had developed a 60 MW breeder at Argonne National Labs called the integral fast reactor (IFR) which ran successfully for years (19-21). It could run either as a breeder or burner. Even as a burner, it has an advantage, that despite its high cost, it can burn any actinide equally, whether it has an even or odd atomic number. In 1994, work on it was abandoned, largely at the instigation of Senator Kerry, who saw it as a proliferation threat. In the section on fusion breeding, the author envisions a role for it in a possible energy architecture based on fusion breeding. In fact, the role we see for it is specifically one that *eliminates* a proliferation threat. Currently the British are seriously considering building a 600 MW version called PRISM (13), which they plan to use to treat their plutonium waste, ie. To reduce their proliferation risk.

References:

1. Helen Raleigh, The West Mimics Mao, Takes a Green Leap Forward, Wall Street Journal, September 21, 2022

https://www.wsj.com/articles/the-west-mimics-mao-takes-a-green-leap-forward-clean-energy-china-communism-farming-industrialization-quota-11663767101?mod=opinion_lead_pos8

2. BP Energy Outlook 2019, https://www.bp.com/content/dam/bp/business-sites/en/global/corporate/pdfs/energy-economics/energy-outlook/bp-energy-outlook-2019.pdf

3. Robert Peltier, *AEP's John W. Turk, Jr. Power Plant Earns* POWER's *Highest Honor,* Power news and technology for the global energy industry, Aug 1, 2013, https://www.powermag.com/aeps-john-w-turk-jr-power-plant-earns-powers-highest-honor/

4. Household Air pollution, WHO document, https://www.who.int/news-room/fact-sheets/detail/household-air-pollution-and-health

5. Martin Hoffert et al. Energy implications of future stabilization of atmospheric CO_2 content. Nature. 1998;395:881.

6. W. Manheimer, American Physics, Climate Change, and Energy, Forum on Physics and society, April 2012

7.   Richard Gray, The true toll of the Chernobyl Disaster, BBC, July, 2019 https://www.bbc.com/future/article/20190725-will-we-ever-know-chernobyls-true-death-toll

8. P. Voosen, *Hiroshima and Nagasaki Cast Long Shadows Over Radiation Science*, New York Times, April 11, 2011

9. M. Tubiana et al., Linear No-threshold relationship is inconsistent with radiation biologic and experimental data. Radiology, **251**(1), 13 April 2009. http://www.ncbi.nlm.nih.gov/pmc/articles/PMC2663584/

10. Radiation Hormesis, Wikipedia https://en.wikipedia.org/wiki/Radiation_hormesis
11. Neil Kapoor, We Have To Go Nuclear, July 2, 2021, Kleinman Center for energy Policy, Harvard University

https://kleinmanenergy.upenn.edu/news-insights/we-have-to-go-nuclear/
12. UK's Boris Johnson goes nuclear with swansong energy investment By M. Muvija and Susanna Twidale, Reuters, September 1, 2022

https://www.reuters.com/business/energy/uk-invest-700-mln-pounds-new-nuclear-plant-pm-johnsons-swansong-2022-09-01/

13. PRISM, by GE Hitachi, https://nuclear.gepower.com/build-a-plant/products/nuclear-power-plants-overview/prism1

14. France drafts law to streamline red tape around nuclear reactor construction, Reuters, September 27, 2022
https://www.reuters.com/business/energy/france-expects-build-first-new-epr2-reactor-before-may-2027-ministry-official-2022-09-27/#:~:text=President%20Emmanuel%20Macron%20has%20put,reduce%20the%20bureaucratic%20processes%20involved.

15. M. I. Hoffert et al., "Advanced technology paths to global climate stability: Energy for a greenhouse planet", *Science*, vol. 298, pp. 981-987, Nov. 2002.

16. J. P. Freidberg and A. C. Kadak, "Fusion–fission hybrids revisited", *Nature Phys.*, vol. 5, pp. 370, Jun. 2009.

17. Joel Guidez, and Sophie Gabriel, Extraction of uranium from sea water, a few facts, EPJ Nuclear Sci. and Technol. 2016 2, 10,

18.R. Garwin, G. Charpak, Megawatts and Megatons (Knopf, Distributed by Random House, New York, 2001)

19.Y. Chang, Advanced fast reactor: a next generation nuclear energy concept. Forum Phys. Soc. (2002)

20.W. Hannum, W. Marsh, G. Stanford, Purex and Pyro are not the Same (Physics and Society, vol 32, 2004)

21.T. Benyon et al., The technology of the integral fast reactor and its associated fuel cycle. Prog. Nucl. Energy 31(1/2) (1997)

22.L. Freeman et al., ''Physics experiments and lifetime performance of the light water breeder reactor,'' Nucl. Sci. Eng., vol. 102, pp. 341–364, Aug. 1989.

23. National Nuclear data center https://www.nndc.bnl.gov/sigma/index.jsp   This web site has a large amount of nuclear data

II. While Climate has changed and always will, the is no climate crisis

The Climate Industrial Complex

This author sees the fear of a climate catastrophe in the next decade or so as simply a mass delusion. It is not so much that the science of it is incorrect, although much of it certainly is. It is the refusal of the anyone, from the highest general to the lowest food soldier of this mass delusion, to tolerate any dissent. For instance in his Dec 30, 2018 show Meet the Press, devoted to climate change, the moderator Chuck Todd said:

"We're not going to debate climate change, the existence of it. The Earth is getting hotter, period. And human activity is a major cause, period. We're not going to give time to climate deniers. The science is settled, even if political opinion is not."

In short, no dissent will be tolerated, just as in the case of a mass delusion. Of course Chuck Todd is not a scientists, but presumably has spoken to some. But has he ever spoken to Richard Lindzen, Roy Spencer, Will Happer, Patrick Moore, Steven Koonin, Judith Curry.......? These are scientists with impeccable reputations and expertise who would give him a very different viewpoint.

Accordingly this author investigates here the motivating factor for the wind and solar transition, namely the fear of CO_2 induced of climate change. In a single sentence this fear is vastly overblown. There is certainly no scientific basis for expecting a climate crisis from too much CO_2 in the atmosphere in the next century or so. Hence there is no reason why civilization cannot advance using both fossil fuel power and nuclear power, gradually shifting to more and more nuclear power.

Richard Lindzen, most likely the worlds foremost authority on geological fluid motion, brilliantly summed up the absurdity of the supposed climate crisis:

"What historians will definitely wonder about in future centuries is how deeply flawed logic, obscured by shrewd and unrelenting propaganda, actually enabled a coalition of powerful special interests to convince nearly everyone in the world that CO_2 from human industry was a dangerous, planet-destroying toxin. It will be remembered as the greatest mass delusion in the history of the world- that CO_2, the life of plants, was considered for a time to be a deadly poison."

Regarding special interests, the skeptics are often accused of being shills for oil and coal companies, but the reality is that the hundreds of billions, no trillions that has gone to the support of climate alarmism supports what Bjorn Lomborg (One of the 100 most influential individuals according to Time Magazine) has called 'The climate industrial complex' (1). It begins:

The tight relationship between the groups echoes the relationship among weapons makers, researchers and the U.S. military during the Cold War. President Dwight Eisenhower famously warned about the might of the "military-industrial complex," cautioning that "the potential for the disastrous rise of misplaced power exists and will persist." He worried that "there is a recurring temptation to feel that some spectacular and costly action could become the miraculous solution to all current difficulties."

This is certainly true of climate change. We are told that very expensive carbon regulations are the only way to respond to global warming, despite ample evidence that this approach does not pass a basic cost-benefit test. We must ask whether a "climate-industrial complex" is emerging, pressing taxpayers to fork over money to please those who stand to gain.

And concluding with:

The partnership among self-interested businesses, grandstanding politicians and alarmist campaigners truly is an unholy alliance. The climate-industrial complex does not promote discussion on how to overcome this challenge in a way that will be best for everybody. We should not be surprised or impressed that those who stand to make a profit are among the loudest calling for politicians to act.

While the media claims the science is settled, there are at least tens of thousands of highly qualified scientists denying this claim (2). Believers argue, "yes, but they are not climate scientists!". Well, what is a climate scientist? The field of 'climate science' is so vast, encompassing physics, chemistry, biology, earth science, mathematics, computer science, agriculture, virtually every field of engineering, that no single person can master even tiny part of it. Realistically nobody is a climate scientist. But let's consider a few examples.

Richard Lindzen is just about the world's leading authority on geophysical fluid dynamics. Is he not a 'climate scientist'? William Happer is about the world's leading authority on the interaction of radiation with complex molecules, the very basis of the greenhouse effect. Is he not a 'climate scientist'? Judith Curry, was the former head of earth science at Georgia Tech, but left the academic world due to its stultifying demands for conformity. Is she not a 'climate scientist'? What about Steven Koonin, one of the world leading physicists, who made discoveries in many areas of physics, and recently wrote a book critical of 'the climate emergency' called 'Unsettled' (3), presumably to mock the claims that the 'science is settled'. What about Bjorn Lomborg, Patrick Moore and Michael Shellenberg, three of the world's leading environmentalists, each of whom has written a book (4-6) denying the climate crisis. Are they not 'climate scientists'? None of these believe we are on the cusp of a 'climate crisis'. Aspects of the detailed physics of climate change can be complex but testing the claims and predictions of the believers is simple. Doing so, one sees that there is neither a climate crisis now nor on the visible horizon.

Actually, one does not have to be a climate expert to contribute to the skepticism. This author, a scientist with more than 50 years of experience, but makes no claim to be a 'climate scientist', has played minor role. One can simply check out the predictions of the prophets of doom against a Google search and see that for the most part these are grossly exaggerated (7). Anyone can do this anywhere, any time, there is no need for a 'climate scientist' to guide us. Furthermore, one can do the same with media reports and conclude that most of the legacy media plays a very one-sided role in its reporting on the climate dilemma (8). Full disclosure: other scientists have criticized this work (9). The author's response to their criticisms is recorded in Ref. (10). Reference (10) lists a large number of climate experts (as opposed to 'climate scientists') who dispute the standard dogma of a climate emergency. While it is a subjective matter, to this author, his list is one of scientists who have far more knowledge, experience, and gravitas regarding the climate dilemma than do most of the scientists who have made a name for themselves by predicting climate gloom and doom. Finally, most of the projections of calamity are made by running numerical simulations of the climate. This is an area in which the author does have considerable experience in his 50+ year career and has pointed out some of the pitfalls of this approach (11) as have many others (3, 12, 13).

This obsession with a false onrushing climate emergency has not only done the obvious harm to the economies of the countries and states that have greatly embraced solar and wind, but it has also done perhaps even more harm in less obvious ways. The mental stress put on children and young adults has hurt them enormously (14-16). They are suffering depression in much greater numbers now, convinced that the world will end in their youth. One can only feel sorry for Greta Thunberg whose childhood was robbed from her by the climate industrial complex. This author is convinced that their actions are nothing short of child abuse.

In fact no less of a source than the White House (17) has given a graph of the increase in mental health problems (depression) in young adults from 12 to over 26. Their graph is shown in Figure (1).

Figure 1. Percent of the population with a major depressive episode in the past year by age, 2008-2020

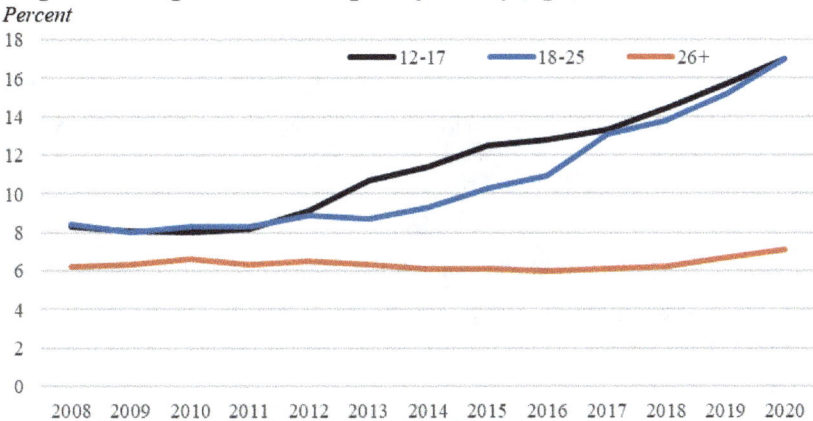

Percent

Source: Substance Abuse and Mental Healthh Services Administration

Figure 1: A graph from the White House showing the increase in depression in children and young adults, the increase coinciding with the time the climate delusion really took over much thinking. Taken from Ref. 17

Who knows whether the cause is due to the climate industrial complex, but the years of increase do match up with the accelerating mass delusion of climate change. Fortunately once someone reaches the age of 26, they apparently have enough sense not to take the propaganda of 'the end of the world by 2030 (see for instance Bernie Sander's 2019 statement in the next subsection) very seriously.

The Chicken Littles of the Climate Industrial Complex

One cannot listen to national and world leaders very long without learning false information that there is a climate crisis which we have very little time to solve. Here are some statements from the Glasgow Nov 2021 international conference on climate change. There are many, many more like this:

"Humanity has long since run down the clock on climate change. It's one minute to midnight on that Doomsday clock and we need to act now." Boris Johnson

"Our addiction to fossil fuels is pushing humanity to the brink. We face a stark choice: Either we stop it — or it stops us. It's time to say: enough." Antonio Guterres, secretary general of UN

"Quite literally it is the last-chance saloon. We must now translate fine words into still finer actions." Prince Charles

"President Biden is committed to cutting greenhouse gas emissions 50-52 percent below 2005 levels in 2030, reaching a 100% carbon pollution-free power sector by 2035, and achieving a net-zero economy by no later than 2050." White house statement November 2021

"The scientific community is telling us in no uncertain terms that we have less than 11 years left to transform our energy system away from fossil fuels to energy efficiency and sustainable energy, if we are going to leave this planet healthy and habitable for ourselves, our children, grandchildren, and future generations." Bernie Sanders presidential campaign 2020 web site

This author, a practicing scientist with over 50 years' experience, gets very nervous on hearing politicians say they are following 'the scientific community'.

This confers on us unanimity which we don't have, and authority on us which we don't want. To me it is basically a way for the politician to say, 'Do what I tell you'.

But should someone have missed these statements by politicians, all one has to do is turn to the New York Times, Washington Post, ABC, CBS, NBC, PBS, MSNBC, or CNN to learn the same thing. No dissent is allowed!

What about scientific journals, do they permit deviations from the orthodoxy? Few skeptical articles are accepted for publication in the most standard journals. Most are published in blogs. Here is a quote from the editorial in Science Magazine, one of the most prestigious scientific journals, by the editor Marcia McNutt (18):

But now with climate change, we face a slowly escalating but long-enduring global threat to food supplies, ...to support a population of more than 7 billion people.

The time for debate has ended. Action is urgently needed.....to reduce their per-capita fossil fuel emissions even further...

But in case anyone still does not get the idea, Dr. McNutt went on to say that skeptics belong in one of the circles of Dante's inferno. Figure 2, is her picture of this from her Science Magazine editorial.

Figure (2): "where [would]...Dante...place all of us who are borrowing against this Earth...?" Dr. McNutt's picture of one of the circles of hell where the skeptics of human induced climate change ought to go. From (18)

If somebody does manage to get over all the hurdles and publish a skeptical article on climate change in one of the major journals, does he or she have a chance of spreading his view on social media?

Here is Face Book's statement November 2021:

We have a responsibility to tackle climate misinformation on our services, which is why we partner with more than 80 independent fact-checking organizations globally to review and rate content, including content about climate change. When they rate content as false, we reduce its distribution so fewer people see it and we show a warning label with more context. And we apply penalties to people who repeatedly share false information.

Here is twitter (this may be changing with Elon Musk possibly taking over the company):

Twitter is banning misleading advertisements that go against the scientific consensus of climate change, the company announced on Friday, which was Earth Day.

"We believe that climate denialism shouldn't be monetized on Twitter, and that misrepresentative ads shouldn't detract from important conversations about the climate crisis," Twitter said in a blog post.

Here is Google (October 2021):

That's why today, we're announcing a new monetization policy for Google advertisers, publishers and YouTube creators that will prohibit ads for, and monetization of, content that contradicts well-established scientific consensus around the existence and causes of climate change. This includes content referring to climate change as a hoax or a scam, claims denying that long-term trends show the global climate is warming, and claims denying that greenhouse gas emissions or human activity contribute to climate change.

What about major scientific societies? Here is the American Physical Society:

Multiple lines of evidence strongly support the finding that anthropogenic greenhouse gases have become the dominant driver of global climate warming observed[2] since the mid-twentieth century[7].

Here is the American Meteorological Society:

"Warming of the climate system now is unequivocal, according to many different kinds of evidence." It goes on to say, "It is clear from extensive scientific evidence that the dominant cause of the rapid change in climate of the past half century is human-induced increases in the amount of atmospheric greenhouse gases ..."

Can all of these authoritative sources be **wrong**? **It seems inconceivable, but they almost certainly are!** Mass delusion reaching deeply into politics, the media, and prestigious scientific societys??

It is particularly disheartening to see these learned scientific societies make such definitive claims when so much contrary information is readily available. They do not even put error bars on their statements! Don't they realize that the radiative forcing from the excess CO_2 in the atmosphere is much less than 1% of the total radiation input, and there are other climate and meteorological effects that are much more dominant? Don't they recognize that for much the last 10,000 years, the earth has almost certainly been warmer than today? Don't they know that there is solid scientific, archaeological, and historical evidence proving this. Don't they know that in those 10,000 years, there have been many oscillations between warm and cold periods, not so different from today's warm period? Don't they realize that in the warm periods, civilization flourished, in the cold periods it suffered? Don't they realize that in its geological history, the earth's temperature and CO_2 varied widely with little correlation to each other? This information, by very well established sources such as NOAA, NASA, The National Hurricane Center, The IPCC ....., is very simple to get on the Google search engine, the very search engine of a company that specifically says it will not provide information on 'claims denying that long-term trends show the global climate is warming'. Don't they realize this? Why didn't they perform these obvious checks before joining the mass delusion? It is not tough to get this information!

Some naked emperors of the climate industrial complex, and others

To start, we consider two naked emperors. We can now compare their predictions of 30 years ago with today's reality. James Hansen, the leader of the Goddard institute at Columbia University, in1988 predicted great warming over the next few decades for a variety of CO_2 atmospheric inputs. The world's actual CO_2 input was greater than his maximum assumption. In Fig. (3) are shown his predictions of temperature rise from 1988 to 2030, and the actual measurements up to 2012 (19).

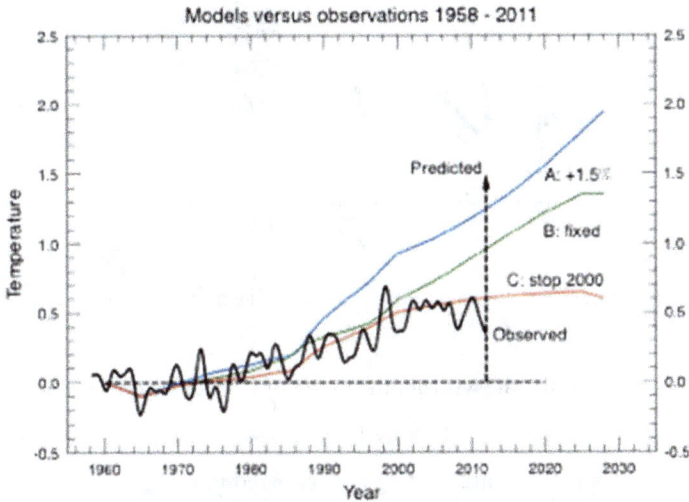

Figure (3) James Hansen's prediction of world temperature rise for various assumptions of CO_2 emission. His maximum case (case A) for CO_2 emission considerably underestimated the actual CO_2 input. The actual temperature rise is shown in black. (19)

Undoubtedly there are new simulations that now give perfect agreement from 1960 to 2020, but predict calamity in the next 10 or 20 years. But how many bites from the apple do the modelers get before they lose all credibility? After all it was John von Neuman who said "With 4 parameters, I can simulate an elephant; with 5, I can get him to wiggle his trunk". All these climate simulations have many more than 5 parameters (12).

In fact a reasonable image of an elephant has been simulated with 4 parameters; it wiggled his trunk with 5 (20). The image of the elephant wiggling his trunk is shown in Figure (4).

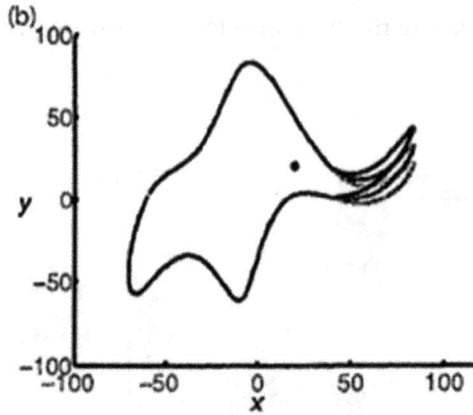

Figure (4): The simulated elephant wiggling his trunk. (20)

Hansen is hardly the only one who got the prediction of future temperature wrong. John Christy (13) presented testimony to congress showing a whole variety of numerical simulations of future heating as compared to reality. The simulations were way off. Figure (5) is from what he presented to congress.

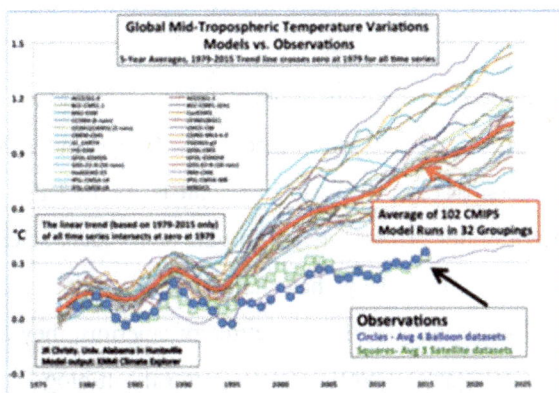

Above: Global average mid-tropospheric temperature variations (5-year averages) for 32 models (lines) representing 102 individual simulations. Circles (balloons) and squares (satellites) depict the observations. The Russian model (INM-CM4) was the only model close to the observations.

Figure (5) from Christy's testimony to congress. (13)

Notice that all of the simulations predicted much greater temperature rise than was actually measured. Since all of the simulations overestimated the temperature, they are not making random errors; if they were, some would underestimate the temperature rise. One cannot escape the conclusion that a bias toward heating is built into all the numerical codes. In fact several people (3, 11, 12, 13) have pointed out the difficulties with these simulations. Yet on the basis of these simulations, which cannot even predict the present, the climate industrial complex is planning to spend trillions to take apart our existing energy infrastructure, and replace it with something that does not even work.

It is interesting, that as Christy points out, there is one curve that got it about right: the Russian model! Russia has had a very strong, independent scientific tradition dating at least since the time of Peter the Great when he set up the Russian Academy of Science. Even during the Communist era, the Academy was as independent of party control as any organization there could be. So how could the Russian modelers have gotten it right when all the western models all got it wrong?

My answer perhaps descends into speculation and might be judged frivolous, but it seems to the author to be well worth recording. In the United States and the west, we do not arrest or execute dissident scientists, as the Russians did under the worst abuses of Stalin. However, we do punish dissident scientists in other ways, we simply cut off or deny their funding and/or their access to major journals. In fact, most vocal skeptics are retired or emeritus; they do not have to worry about their next grant, and they publish mostly in blogs. It is unlikely Russia has the same worry about climate change that we do. Perhaps Russian scientists do not have to 'tune' their codes to obtain politically correct results.

It does not always take 30 years to expose an incorrect prediction. In 2008 Hansen predicted that there would be no summer time Arctic ice after 5 or 10 years (21). In Figure (6) are shown NOAA measurements of Arctic ice in March (the maximum) and September (the minimum) (22).

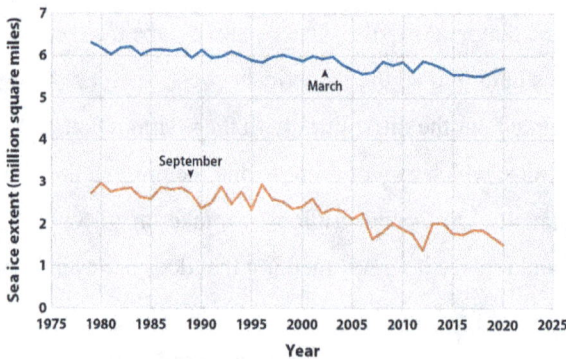

Figure (6). The actual measured extent of Arctic ice as a function of year from 1979 to 2020 in March (the maximum) and September (the minimum). Had Hansen made his prediction in 2007 instead of 2008, for 2018 instead of 2020, the actual summer ice would have increased! (21)

Another well established scientist who missed on an important prediction is Professor Kerry Emanuel of MIT. He had recently been celebrated (23) for his study that the warming of the ocean would make hurricanes more frequent and intense:

Besides unraveling the mechanisms of how hurricanes develop, Emanuel was the first to link them with the warming of sea surface waters driven by climate change. His models currently predict a 5% increase in hurricane intensity, i.e., wind speed, for each one degree rise in ocean temperatures.

However Figure (7) is a plot from NOAA of the ocean surface temperature over the last century and a half (24).

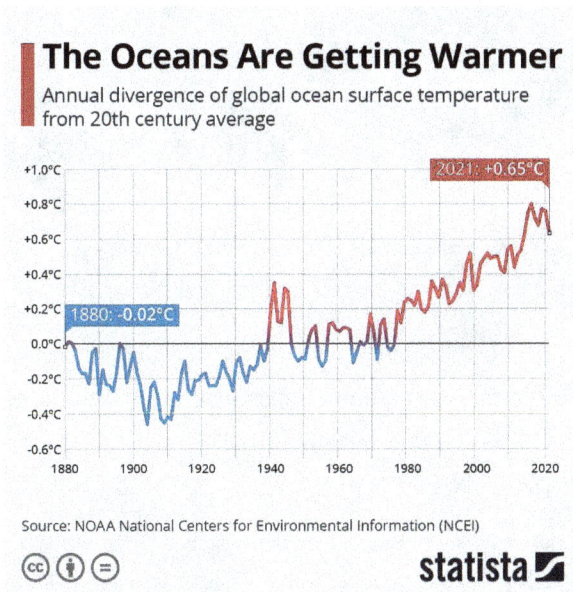

The Oceans Are Getting Warmer
Annual divergence of global ocean surface temperature from 20th century average

Source: NOAA National Centers for Environmental Information (NCEI)

statista

Figure (7): A plot of ocean surface temperature over the last 140 years from NOAA, showing that in the last 60 years the oceans have warmed by ~ 1°C. Professor Emanuel's prediction is the this should have given a significant increase in hurricane frequency and intensity. (24)

Figure (8) is a plot from NOAA (25) of the number of strong hurricanes striking the American East coast over this time period.

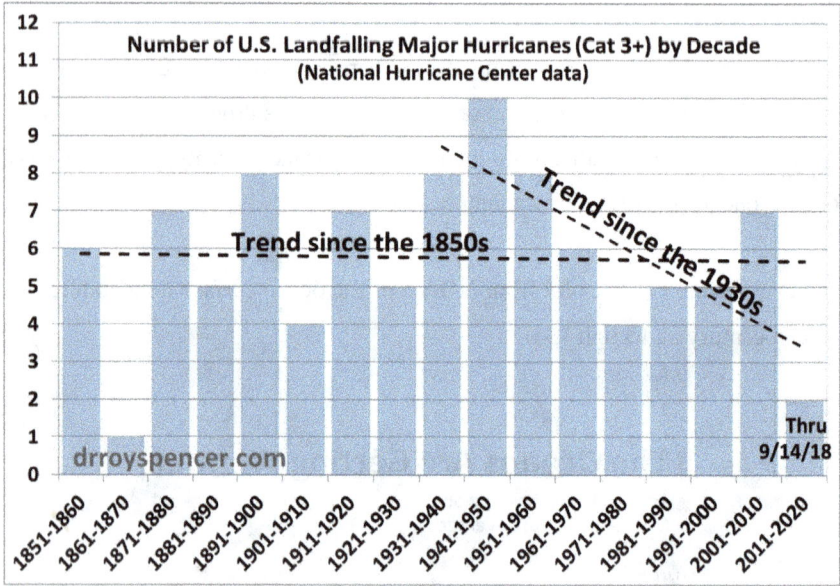

Figure (8): A NOAA plot of the number of intense hurricanes striking the US over the last 140 years. (25)

Clearly the number of strong hurricanes striking the US has been decreasing from the 1950's to the present, as the ocean has warmed, This is just exactly the opposite of what Professor Emanuel predicted.

Another NOAA measurement is the relative total energy going into hurricanes over the decades (26). This includes wind speed, size, and time duration of the storm. This may well be a more direct test of Professor Emanuel's hypothesis. NOAA has such measurements for over 140 years. The graph is shown in Figure (9).

Accumulated Cyclone Energy
Combined numbers, intensity, and duration - 1878 to 2020

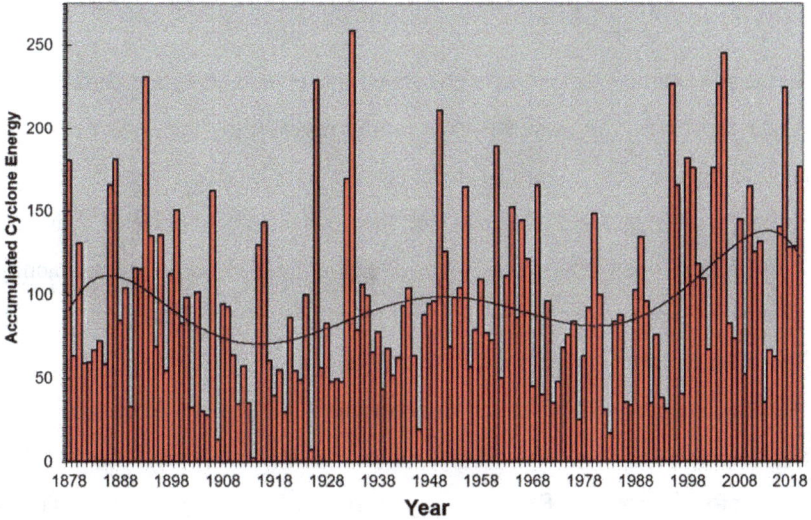

Figure 9 : The relative energy in Atlantic hurricanes from 1878 to 2020, as recorded by NOAA. The black line is an average smoothed value. Clearly there is a ~ 50 year oscillation. Perhaps there is a slight increase over the last 20 years. (26)

Professor Emanuel and the skeptics can both take some comfort from Fig. (9). While there has been some increase in total hurricane energy in about the last 20 years, the current averaged peak is not that much greater than the one in about 1885. There is certainly no indication of any kind of climate crisis.

Now we consider some emperors still wearing clothes. In 2006, 32,000 scientists, including 9000 Ph.D's signed a petition disputing the believer's view of the climate (2). The petition was led by none other than Fred Seitz, at the time the president of the National Academy of Science (NAS). In 2022 a new organization, Clintel has formed and has put out a similar statement (2). Already over 1200 professional scientist from all over the world have signed on. This certainly contradicts the assertion that "the science is settled'. In fact, if, as publicized, 97% of scientists really believe the current dogma on climate change, and the signers represent the 3% who presumably do not, we would have expected to see a petition supporting this view signed by ~970,000 scientists, ~300,000 with Ph.D's.

While the raw number scientists who signed these statements are certainly an important data point, this author is even more impressed by the quality of some of the leading skeptics. Some of these are Richard Lindzen (world's leading expert on geophysical fluid dynamics and the youngest person elected to NAS), William Happer (one of the world's world leading authorities on the interaction of radiation with atoms and molecules, and inventor of the sodium guide star, an earth based method of correcting for atmospheric turbulence in large telescopes, and leading member of NAS), Roy Spencer and John Christy (in charge of the NOAA/NASA/UAH space based temperature data collection. Christy has testified before congress), Patrick Moore (originator of Greenpeace, resigned when he thought it became too extreme, he recently wrote a book critical of the climate alarmism, and has testified several time before congress), Judith Curry (former chairwoman of the earth an atmospheric science department at Georgia Tech but resigned from her academic post when the academic atmosphere became too stultifying for her), Ivar Giaever (Nobel Prize winner in physics, resigned from the American Physical Society because of its stand on climate change), Steven Koonin (one of today's leading physicists, he also recently wrote a book; to mock the claim of the alarmists that 'the science is settled', he titled his book 'Unsettled'[3]), Patrick Michaels (Retired from the atmospheric department of the University of Virginia, and chief Virginia climatologist), Michael Shellenberger (leading environmentalist and originator of Environmental Progress, also wrote a book criticizing climate alarmism), Mark Mills (the leading energy expert of the Manhattan Institute). Then there a few more who are no longer with us. Foremost there is Fred Seitz (former head of the Rockefeller University and former president of the National Academy of Science), Fred Singer, (retired professor University of Virginia, designed many of the space-based instruments used for environmental measurements), Freeman Dyson (long time scholar at Princeton Institute of Advanced Studies, probably the greatest physicist who has NOT won a Nobel Prize), and many, many others.

This author certainly has respect for both Kerry Emanuel and James Hansen. They played in the arena as best they could and certainly contributed a lot to their field of endeavor. I certainly do not point to their wrong predictions with any sense of superiority, having made several wrong predictions in my own corner of the scientific world. However unlike those of Emanuel and Hansen, nobody is wasting trillions on mine. Perhaps those making predictions should act with less hubris, and pay a bit more attention to Yogi Berra's timeless wisdom: "Predictions are tough, especially about the future".

A brief tour of CO_2 induced radiation forcing in the atmosphere

To continue we take a look at the physics of CO_2 in the atmosphere. If there is one CO_2 molecule and radiation coming up from the earth hits it at the right frequency, the molecule absorbs some radiation, gets into an excited state, nearly immediately decays and reradiates, sending some of that radiation back to earth. If there are many CO_2 molecules, the temptation might be to simply add up the heating from each molecule, but that is incorrect. For one thing, no matter how many molecules there are, it can never reradiate in that frequency range more than a black body would at that temperature. In other word, the radiation at that frequency can saturate.

To calculate what is called a CO_2 driven radiative forcing, one needs a start date and a final date (or equivalently an initial CO_2 concentration and a final concentration). One then calculates the added radiation coming down to earth, in W/m^2 from this added concentration. The IPCC calculaiton is shown in their Sixth Assessment report (27). Their Figure 2.10, reproduced as our Fig (8), gives their calculated radiative forcing from 1900 (CO_2 concentration of ~280 ppm) to 2020 (~420 ppm); a forcing of ~$1.75 W/m^2$.

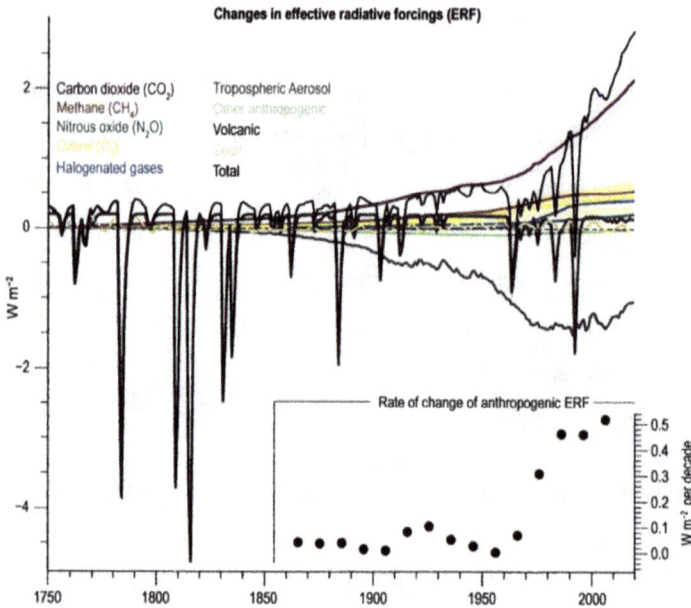

Figure (8) Calculated CO_2 and other greenhouse gas forcing as reported in the IPCC 6th assessment report. Their CO_2 forcing from 1900 to 2020 is about $1.75 W/m^2$. (27)

Recently, Wijngaarden and Happer (28) have made an extremely detailed calculation of the radiation transport considering the 5 most common greenhouse gas atmospheric impurities. Their main results are shown as Fig. (9). The smooth blue curve is the black body radiation of the earth at 287 degrees Kelvin. This is what the earth would radiate back to space if the atmosphere had no effect. The greenhouse gases tend to make the actual curve lower than the black body curve, meaning that the earth is reabsorbing some of its radiation, heating the planet. The green curve is the radiation with all greenhouse gases except CO_2 present. The black curve is the radiation with 400 parts per million of CO_2, approximately today's concentration. The red curve is the radiation if the CO_2 concentration were doubled.

56

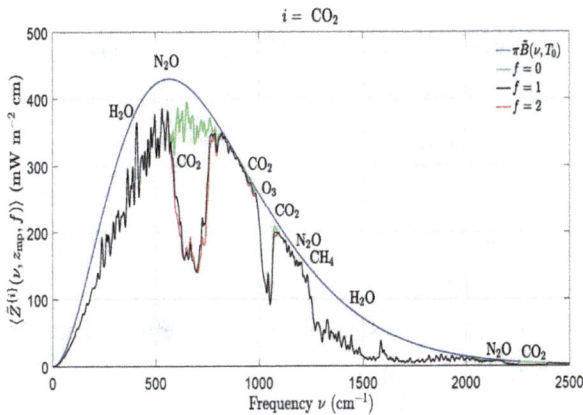

Figure (9): The Planck radiation curve (blue), with all greenhouse gases except CO_2 (green), with today's concentration of CO_2 (400 ppm, black) and with double today's concentration (800 ppm, red). (28)

W&H find a radiative forcing of ~3 W/m^2. The W&H calculation and the IPCC calculations cover different time periods, or equivalently, different initial and final CO_2 calculations, so it is difficult to determine the extent to which they agree or disagree. For our purposes here, we will use the W&H calculation, as it is a more detailed one. Among other things W&H developed numerical algorithms allowing them to examine and analyze individually, hundreds of thousands of molecular rotational and vibrational states using only a PC. In any case, the scientists (27,28) are basically on the same page, it is the politicians and media personnel that have wildly different interpretations. Depending on their assumptions, W&H calculate a temperature increase on the earth surface of 1-2°C, depending on their assumptions.

Let us consider the radiative forcing as compared to the total radiation from the sun impinging on the upper atmopsher of the earth. This is ~1000W/m^2. However averaging over night and day, an average might be something more like half of this. Hence we can very roughly estimate the forcing as 0.3-0.6% of the incident solar radiation. One might reasonably think that a radiative forcing of ~

0.3-0.6% of the incident solar radiation, and a 1-2°K temperature increase which is ~ 0.3-0.6% of the Kelvin temperature of 300°K, are reasonably consistent with one another. In fact it is probably an overestimate to the temperature rise, since the radiation increases as temperature to the fourth power, or the temperature increases as the fourth root of the radiation. In fact, Figure 114 of (29) gives Lamb's graph predicting that increasing CO_2 in the atmosphere from 400-800 parts per million would increase the earth temperature by ~1.5°C, not far off of the W&H estimate. Lamb does discuss the warming effect of atmospheric CO_2, but not until page 330, hardly a claim that it is a dominant driver of temperture. Reference (29) has long been considered the primary textbook on climate science. In joining the climate mass delusion here, scientific societies ignored it, as we will see with this and other examples

If the world keeps using fossil fuel at 10 TW, as it does today, this adds about 2 ppm of CO_2 to the atmosphere per year. In other words it would take 200 years to double the CO_2 concentration and increase the temperature by a degree or two. However long before that, the world hopefully will make a transition to nuclear power, perhaps fueled by fusion breeding (30). In no case is it 'one minute to midnight' (Boris Johnson), nor are we in the 'last chance saloon' (Prince Charles).

However truly the amazing thing is that the forcing as calculated by the IPCC scientists (the believers) and as calculated by W&H (the skeptics) are not that different. The scientists basically agree, and also agree with Lamb (29). In fact, had they calculated the forcing over the same time periods (i.e. same initial and final atmospheric CO_2 concentrations), who knows how close their calculations would have been, perhaps they would have gotten very nearly the same result. It is strictly a matter of different predictions from similar results. The IPCC bureaucrats predict that a forcing of 0.3-0.6% will cause a calamity. The skeptics predict that a forcing of 0.3-0.6% will cause something more like a 0.3-06%

temperature rise on the Kelvin scale, namely 1 to 2°C. To this author, the latter prediction seems much more reasonable.

In fact given the space based temperature measurements of the lower atmosphere over the past ~ 45 years, one can very, very roughly test the effect of the CO_2 forcing. Figure 10 is a measurent of this temperature (31) from 1979 (CO_2 concentration of ~ 335 ppm) to 2022 (~415ppm), or a increase of 80ppm.

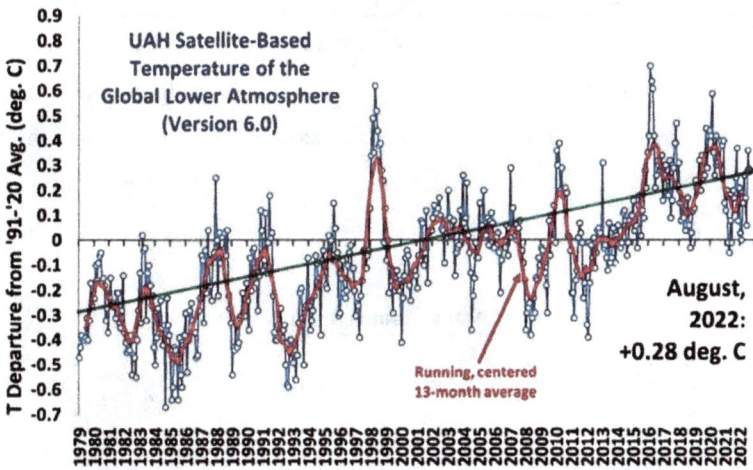

Figure (10) The space based temperature measurement of the lower atmosphere, along with a green line of a rough linear fit, drawn in by the author. (31)

Clearly in this period the temperature, averaged over many fluctuations, has increased by ~ 0.6°C, or ~0.2% of the temperature on the Kelvin scale. The IPCC estimated a forcing of 1.75W/m² with a 140 ppm increase, or ~ 1 W/m² with an 80 ppm increase, or about a 0.1-0.2% increase. This all seems to hang together.

Of course Figure 10 cannot be taken as confirmation of W&H's estimate of 1-2 degrees. The atmosphere is much too complicated to be described by simply the

CO2 content. Figure (11) gives NOAA measurements of world temperature from ~1880 to ~2015, based on ground station measurements from stations around the world.

However NOAA has had problems with its ground based temperature measurements. First of all, in some ways they are more difficult than space based measurements. Space based measurements use a single suite of instruments in a satellite. They give a nearly instantaneous measurements of the entire world's temperature. The ground based measurements have to use, and average in some way, the readings of thousands of stations, many of them in parts of the world where NOAA has no access, many in places not so friendly with the United States. Then NOAA has to be sure they are properly calibrated to one another. Nevertheless, up to ~2015 , NOAA published the temperature graph shown in Fig (11).

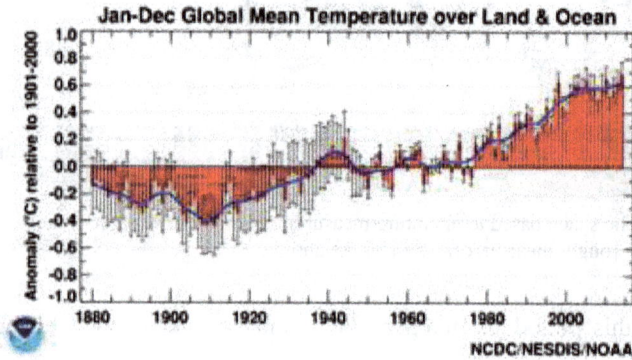

Jan-Dec Global Mean Temperature over Land & Ocean

NCDC/NESDIS/NOAA

Figure (11) A NOAA graph of the world temperature taken before 2020. In 2020 it still figured promonently on a Google Images search. Notice the NOAA icon on the graph.

The graph showed a plateau of world temperature from about 1998 to about 2020. However at this point, NOAA discovered that it had made an error in showing the constant temperature in the 20 years between 1998 and 2015. Then it published a different graph, much more pleasing to its political bosses at the time. This is shown in Fig. (12). Notice that where Fig (11) uses a Centigrade temperature scale, Fig. (12) uses Fahrenheit.

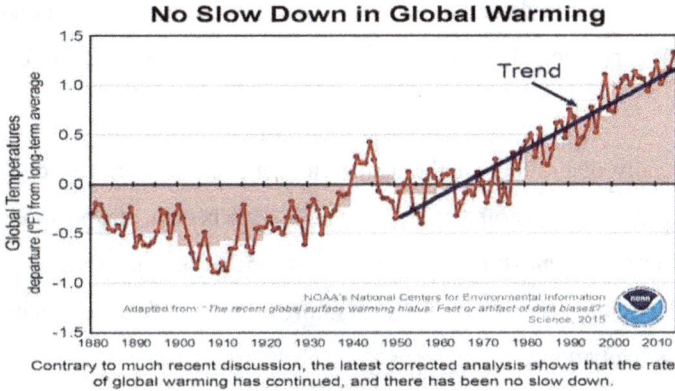

Figure (12)   NOAA's 'revised' temperature graph. Notice once again the NOAA icon on the graph.

The problem is which one should you believe, Fig (11) which stood the test of time with little controversy, or Fig. (12) which generated enormous controversy with congressmen demanding answers and NOAA refusing to provide them? However notice that both measurements show a temperature increase of ~0.6°C between about 1910 and 1940 when there was little increase in atmospheric CO_2; just a little less than the temperature rise between about 1960 and 2000 when atmospheric CO_2 was significantly rising.

This author believes that this sudden reversal on NOAA's part represents a serious problem for this part of the agency. NOAA had initially refused to make its data and new methodology publicly available (32,33), asserting: "Because the confidentiality of these communications among scientists is essential to frank discourse among scientists, those documents were not provided to the Committee," the agency said. "It is a long-standing practice in the scientific community to protect the confidentiality of deliberative scientific discussions."

This author has been a practicing scientist for over 50 years, and this is the first he had ever heard of confidentiality of deliberative scientific discussions. Are we doctors, lawyers or priests all of a sudden? This 'confidentially' is especially inappropriate because these 'discussions' could have a major impact on the lives of billions of people. Shouldn't they know what the experts are forcing down their throats and why?

It is especially disturbing for this author to see such behavior by civil service scientists in a major government lab. The author has been in that position 33 years as a civil service scientist; and as a consultant for the same lab for 20 years. The civil service scientific labs sacrifice *everything*, if the sacrifice their credibility, as NOAA has likely done.

Probably it is better to believe the space-based temperature measurements, and the ground-based measurements taken by other technically advanced countries.

All of this, these theories, and the measurements certainly do not support the assertion of a rapidly approaching climate crisis.

Climate change over the period of human civilization

Let us now consider the temperature record for about 10,000 years, the time of human civilization. When believers say that this or that is a record heat spell, or hurricane, or whatever, they are talking about one particular place, and only during the time official records were kept, perhaps a bit more than a century. However civilization goes way further back than that, and other measurements indicate oscillating hot and cold periods, with many hot periods warmer than today's. Skeptics tend to look over much longer periods of time.

One way of measuring this temperatures in previous eras is with the ratio of ^{18}O to ^{16}O in the Greenland ice cores. About 0.1% of oxygen on earth is the heavier isotope. Water containing the heavier and lighter oxygen isotopes evaporate at a slightly different rates, a difference dependent on temperature (29). Hence measuring the isotope ratio as a function of depth in the ice caps (i.e. as a function of year) gives a very good indication of temperature as a function of year. This is not a local Greenland measurement. The snow on Greenland is from ocean evaporation over a large part of the earth south and west of Greenland. It comes from water evaporated from the tropics and midlatitudes and carried by the prevailing westerly winds, and then carried up to the northern latitudes by general circulation. Hence it is an indication of the average temperature over a large patch of earth at those times.

Graphs of this ratio abound in a Google images search. Most are very choppy (34), but some also average over the rapid time oscillations (35) and normalize the isotope ratio to temperature. One of these is in Figure 13.

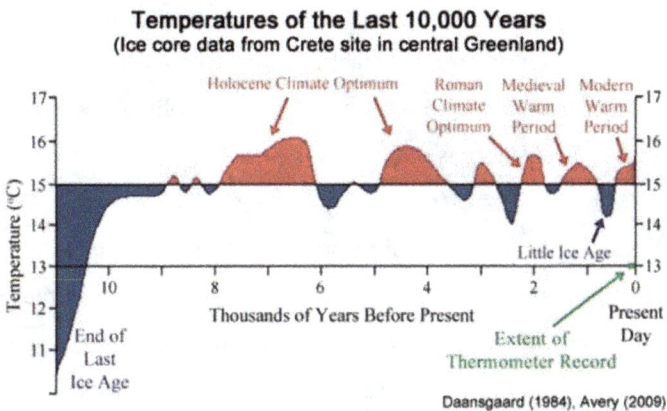

Figure (13): A smoothed plot of average temperature over the last 10,000 years as measured by the Greenland ice caps. (35)

Note that this graph was from a *Google* search; a search from the very organization that claimed that they are "announcing a new monetization policy (which)….prohibits ads for, and monetization of, content that contradicts well-established scientific consensus around the existence and causes of climate change. This includes content ....denying that long-term trends show the global climate is warming, and claims denying that greenhouse gas emissions or human activity contribute to climate change".

Google's Figure (13) certainly denies 'that that long-term trends show the global climate is warming'. On the contrary, it shows that for the period human civilization existed on earth, the climate bounced back and forth between warm and cold periods. It is no coincidence that civilization advanced in the warm periods and decayed in the cold periods.

A source of a great deal of information contradicting the climate emergency dogma can be found on the web site of the CO_2 coalition (34), a small organization of senior scientists, engineers, and other professionals. The organization is united in its belief that there is no climate emergency, atmospheric carbon dioxide is essential for life on earth and its increase so far has, if anything, been beneficial; and the wind and solar cannot be viable power sources to support modern civilization. Other than that, for instance as regarding politics, the members are all over the place. This author is proud to be a member.

As convincing as Figure 13 is, it is far from the only evidence that these earlier warm periods were warmer than today. Figure 14 is a plot of most of the northern hemisphere showing the northernmost limits of forest 4000 years ago, in the Holocene Climate Optimum, about the time of the biblical exodus; and today (29). Remnants of these northern forests from 4000 years ago are still in place and can be examined today. Again, it is obviously not a local measurement. 4000 years ago these forests extended ~ 200 miles further north than they do today, indicating a considerably warmer climate then. Lamb has several similar examples, for instance remnants of forests at higher altitude on mountains, forests that cannot exist at these altitudes today. Lamb's book is perhaps the most well known textbook on the science of the climate; he is often regarded as the father of climate science. He does, in fact discuss the warming effect of atmospheric CO_2, but not until page 330! His estimate of the effect of raising the concentration to 800 ppm is roughly the same as that calculated by Wijngaarden and Happer (28). How can prestigious major scientific societies participate in such a mass deliusion by ignoring the premier textbook in this field, and come up with statements which the textbook soundly contradicts,? Posterity will not look kindly on today's actions of these scientific societies.

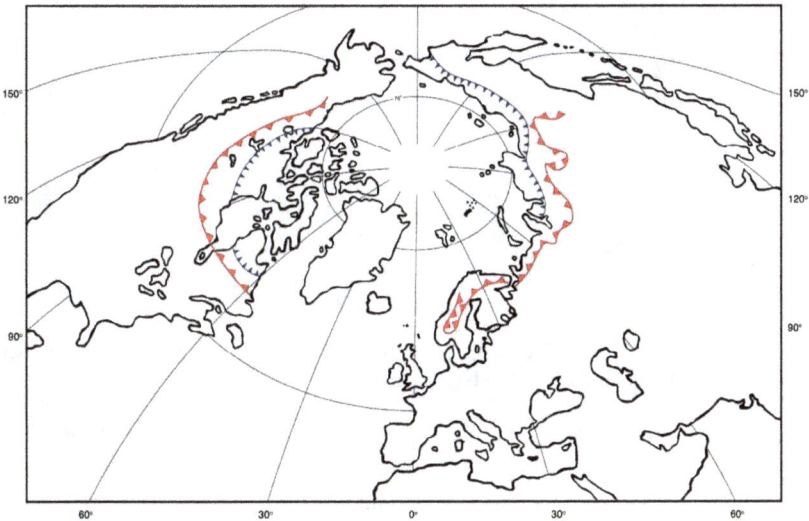

Figure (14): The smaller blue triangles are the limits of northernmost forest 4000 years ago during the Holocene climate optimum; and the larger red triangles, today. Clearly the Holocene climate was sufficiently warmer than today, so that the forests could exist ~ 200 miles further north. Redrawn from Figure 46 of (29).

Another example is the confirmed fact, established from both Roman historical records and archaelogical discoveries, that in the Roman Climate Optimum, the Romans had vineyards all over England (36), extending up to Hadrian's wall. The map in Figure 15 shows places where Roman pruning hooks, used in vineyards, were excavated in England. Also it shows where the remnants of six Roman vineyards were found. Virtually all the literature on Roman wine in England point out that Britain then was considerably warmer than today. Grapes that survive now in say Quebec or Minnesota today are newer hybrid grapes, bred to thrive in cold climate (37).

Roman Vineyard Locations
1. North Thoresby, Lincolnshire
2. Wilby Way, Northants.
3. Wollaston, Northants.
4. Grendon, Northants.
5. Fen Drayton, Cambridgeshire
6. Stanton Low, Bucks.

KEY

Suspected Roman Vineyards

● Pruning hook finds

100 km

Figure (15): A map of England showing where the Roman's grew wine 2000 years ago, when England had a warmer climate than today. (36)

Finally, in the Medieval Warm Period, the Vikings settled Greenland and for hundreds of years, grew barley there, something not possible to do today. Modern explorers found some of this barley in Greenland firmly establishing that it was grown there ~ 1000 years ago (38). Figure 16 shows recently excavated remnants of 1000 year old barley grain found in in Greenland in 2012. Certainly Greenland today is much too cold for cultivating barley.

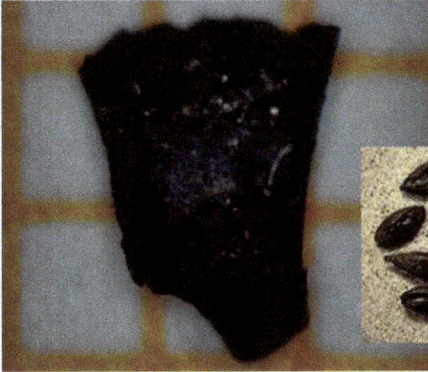

Each grain of barley is only a couple of millimetres long, and the grain weighs less than 0.01 mg – yet the find is now regarded as an archaeological sensation.
Photos: Peter Steen Henriksen

Figure (16): Remnants 1000 year old of barley excavated in Greenland in 2012, planted at a time when Greenland was much warmer than today (38).

In other words, there were much warmer periods than today during the course of human civilization, and these during periods civilization flourished; the in between cold periods were generally disastrous. How can learned scientific societies neglect these well established facts?

Climate over a geological time scale

Finally we take a very brief look at the geological history of temperature and CO_2 on earth. Again, graphs abound on the internet, and the further back one goes, the more speculative they become. A typical example is the graph in Figure 17 (39). There are other similar plots in a simple internet search.

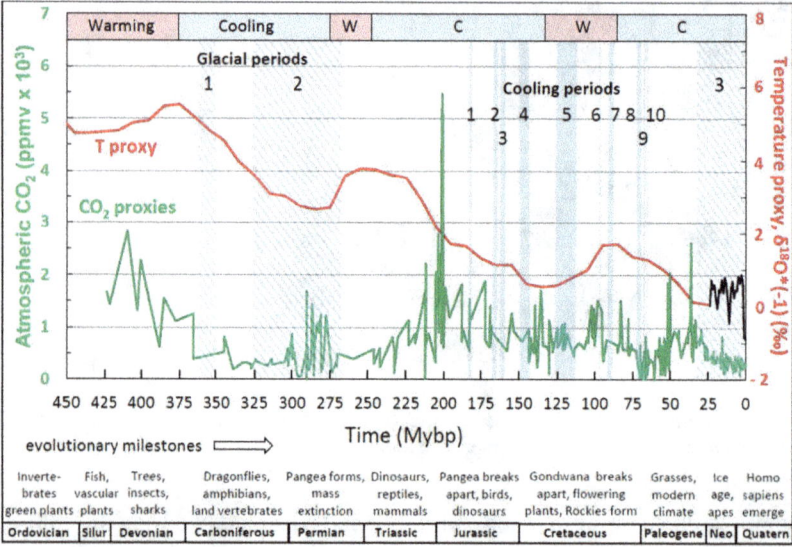

Figure (17): The geological history of CO₂ level and temperature proxy for the past 400 million years. CO2 levels now are ~ 400ppm. (39)

Davis also showed a scatter plot of temperature versus atmospheric CO_2 level reproduced as Figure 18.

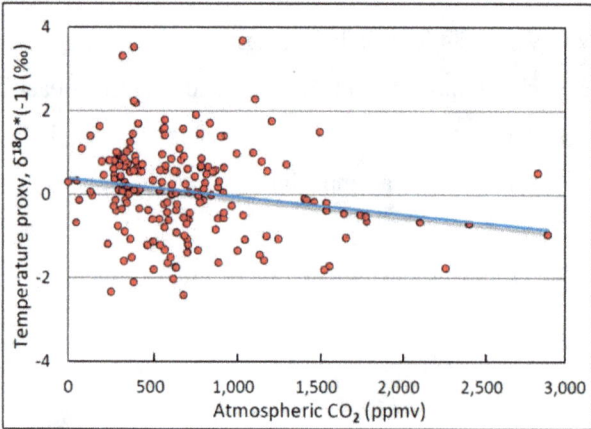

Figure (18): Scatter plot of the correlation of CO_2 level with temperature proxy from Davis. Clearly he finds that the temperature and CO_2 level are basically uncorrelated. In fact using a least square plot, he find a slight negative correlation. (39)

While one may think the geological history has little to do with today, there is one way in which it might be relevant. One of the main fears the climate change believers enunciate is that with the added CO_2, the polar caps in Greenland and Antarctica might melt, raising ocean levels by many meters. However the Antarctica polar cap was formed ~ 40 million years ago (40). Then the earth's temperature was ~8 degrees higher and the CO_2 was about double what is is today. The Greenland ice caps were formed ~ 3 million years ago (41),when the earth's temperature was ~ a degree or two warmer than today and the CO_2 level was ~ 500ppm. This data may not prove that added CO_2 will not melt the ice caps today, but it certainly does not enhance the case it they will.

What an internet search says about climate change

Scientific examination of geological fluid motion, or radiation transport, or scientific examination of isotope ratios, or archaeological and historical records are not the only way to debunk the case that we are now at a time of extreme peril due to climate change. There is something any layman can do. After, let's say after a strong tornado, a politician (7) or a media figure (8) says that these strong tornados are a certain indication of a quickly approaching catastrophe due to climate change. Simply do a Google or Bing search. Almost invariably, it will show that the claim is wildly exaggerated. For example, let's take Dr. Mc Nutt's assertion of a coming world food crisis. Go to Google Images and type in 'graph of world food production' and out will pop many, many graphs, nearly all showing, in different ways, increasing food production. An example is in Figure 19. It shows *per capita* food production, so to get the actual increase in food production, one would have to multiply by the increase in population.

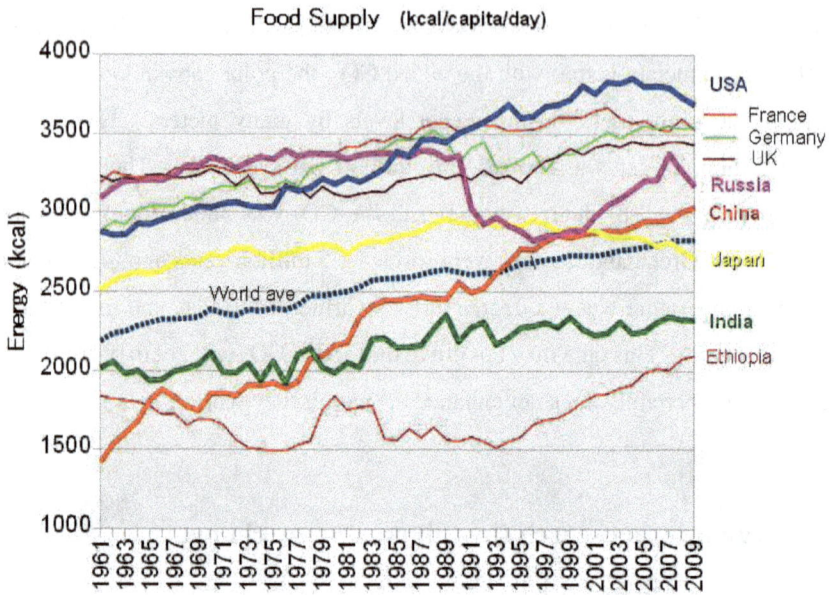

Food Supply (kcal/capita/day)

Figure (19): Per capita food production in kcal/(per-capita per day) from 1961 to 2009, from a simple Google search. Notice that there is a steadily increasing production, with no sign of any 'slowly escalating but long-enduring global threat to food supplies.'

This author's experience is that virtually all of your searches will debunk the claims of imminent catastrophe.

References

1. Bjorn Lomborg, *The Climate-Industrial Complex*, Wall Street Journal, May 22, 2009

2. . www.petitionproject.org   https://clitel.org/world-climate-declaration/

3. Steven E Koonin, *Unsettled, what climate science tells us, what it doesn't, and why it matters* Ben Bella Books, 2021

4. Bjorn Lomborg, False Alarm, How climate change panic costs us trillions, hurts the poorl and fails to fix the planet, Basic Books, 2020

5. Patrick Moore, *Fake invisible catastrophes and threats of doom,* Ecoscience, published by Amazon, 2021

6. Michael Shellenberger, *Apocalypse never, why environmental alarmism hurts us all,* , Harper Collins, 2020

7. Wallace Manheimer, Original sin, prophets, witches, communists, preschool sex abuse, and climate change, International Journal of Engineering and Applied Sciences (IJEAS) ISSN: 2394-3661, Volume-4, Issue-7, July 2017

https://www.ijeas.org/download_data/IJEAS0407025.pdf

8. Wallace Manheimer, Climate change, on media perceptions and misperceptions, Forum of Physics and Society,(American Physical Societal essay journal) October, 2019

https://www.aps.org/units/fps/newsletters/201910/climate-change.cfm

9. Seaver Wang and Zeke Hausfather, Climate Change: Robust Evidence of Causes and Impacts, Comment on my FPS essay, Forum on Physics and Society, January 2020 https://engage.aps.org/fps/resources/newsletters/january-2020

10. Wallace Manheimer, Media, Politics and Climate Change, a response to Wang and Hausfather,Forum on Physics and Society, April 2020 https://www.aps.org/units/fps/newsletters/202004/media.cfm

11. Wallace Manheimer, Some dilemmas of climate simulations wattsupwiththtat, April 27, 2020 https://wattsupwiththat.com/2020/04/27/some-dilemmas-of-climate-simulations/

12. Paul Vossen, , *Climate scientists open their black boxes to scrutiny,* Science, October 28, 2016, volume 354, Issue 6311, p401

13. Christy, John, testimony before congress, February 2016, https://docs.house.gov/meetings/SY/SY00/20160202/104399/HHRG-114-SY00-Wstate-ChristyJ-20160202.pdf

14. Burke, S.E.L., Sanson, A.V. & Van Hoorn, J. The Psychological Effects of Climate Change on Children. *Curr Psychiatry Rep* **20**, 35 (2018). https://doi.org/10.1007/s11920-018-0896-9

15. https://www.hsph.harvard.edu/c-change/subtopics/climate-change-and-mental-health/

16. Fritze, J.G., Blashki, G.A., Burke, S. *et al.* Hope, despair and transformation: Climate change and the promotion of mental health and wellbeing. *Int J Ment Health Syst* **2**, 13 (2008). https://doi.org/10.1186/1752-4458-2-13

17. Reducing the Economic Burden of Unmet Mental Health Needs, The White House, May 31, 2022 https://www.whitehouse.gov/cea/written-materials/2022/05/31/reducing-the-economic-burden-of-unmet-mental-health-needs/

18. Marcia McNutt, Science Magazine, July 3, 2015, editorial

19. Watts, Anthony, *James Hansen's climate forecast of 1988: a whopping 150% wrong*, https://wattsupwiththat.com, June 15, 2012

20. Mayer, J, K. Khairy, and J. Howard, *Drawing an elephant with four complex parameters*, Am. J. Phys. 78, 648, 2010

21. Predictions of climate change gloom and doom

https://www.ehso.com/climatechange-predictions-doom-and-gloom.php

22. Antarctic Ice Sheet, https://en.wikipedia.org/wiki/Antarctic_ice_sheet
23. BBVA foundation, tribute to Kerry Emanuel
https://www.frontiersofknowledgeawards-fbbva.es/noticias/the-bbva-foundation-recognizes-kerry-emanuel-for-detecting-and-predicting-the-intensification-of-hurricanes-as-a-consequence-of-climate-change/
24. Buchholz, Katharina, *Statistica Climate Change*, Jun 8, 2022

https://www.statista.com/chart/19418/divergence-of-ocean-temperatures-from-20th-century-average/

25. NOAA Graph, https://www.ncei.noaa.gov/access/monitoring/monthly-report/global/202113
26. Chris Landsea and Eric Blake [1], Inside the Eye. An incredibly busy hurricane season, NOAA Blog,   https://noaanhc.wordpress.com/2021/06/30/was-2020-a-record-breaking-hurricane-season-yes-but/
27. IPCC Sixth Assessment Report, Chapter 2,
Climate Change 2021: The Physical Science Basis - IPCC
https://www.ipcc.ch/report/ar6/wg1/

28. Wijngaarden, W. A. and W. Happer, Dependence of Earth's Thermal Radiation on Five Most Abundant Greenhouse Gases , https:arXiv.org/pdf/2006.030098.pdf, June 2020

29. Lamb, H. H. *Climate history and the modern world, second edition,* Routledge Publishers, New York and London, 1995
30. Manheimer , Wallace, (2022) *Civilization Needs Sustainable Energy – Fusion Breeding May Be Best,* Journal of Sustainable Development,   Volume 15,   page 98, 2022 https://ccsenet.org/journal/index.php/jsd/article/view/0/46729
31. Spencer, Roy, (2018) *Graph of hurricanes striking the United States,*
https://www.drroyspencer.com/2018/09/u-s-major-landfalling-hurricanes-down-50-since-the-1930

32. Wallace Manheimer, Original sin, prophets, witches, communists, preschool sex abuse, and climate change, International Journal of Engineering and Applied Sciences (IJEAS), Sec 6.6, ISSN: 2394-3661, Volume-4, Issue-7, July 2017

https://www.ijeas.org/download_data/IJEAS0407025.pdf

33. Jeff Tollefson, Nature News October 28, 2015, http://www.nature.com/news/us-science-agency-refuses-request-for- climate-records-1.18660

34. https://co2coalition.org/facts/temperatures-have-changed-for-800000-years-it-wasnt-us/, see also www.co2coalition.org

35.. McVetanovic, *Climate Change- A Geological Perspective*,   Good earth energy blog, March 30,2016, https://www.fortitudeenergyconsultants.rocks/climate-change-a-geological-perspective/;
36. Brown, A. G., I. Meadows, S.D. Turner & D.J. Maitingly, Roman vineyards in Britain: stratigraphic and palynological data from Wollaston in the Nene Valley, England, Antiquity, 75 2001 1: 745-57, https://core.ac.uk/download/pdf/27661.pdf

37. Perry, Leonard, *Cold Climate Grapes*, University of Vermont Extension Department of Plant and Soil Science,
https://pss.uvm.edu/ppp/articles/grapes.html#:~:text=With%20potential%20for%20growing %20in,www.lincolnpeakvineyard.com).

38. Viking Barley in Greenland, Ancient Foods, February 17, 2012,
https://ancientfoods.wordpress.com/2012/02/17/viking-barley-in-greenland/

39. Davis, W. Jackson, *The Relationship between Atmospheric Carbon Dioxide Concentration and Global Temperature for the Last 425 Million Years*
Climate 2017, *5*(4), 76;
https://www.researchgate.net/publication/320123470_The_Relationship_between_Atmospher ic_Carbon_Dioxide_Concentration_and_Global_Temperature_for_the_Last_425_Million_Ye ars

40. Antarctic Ice Sheet, https://en.wikipedia.org/wiki/Antarctic_ice_sheet

41. Chavez, Holly, *How and when did Greenland become covered with ice, Oceanwide expeditions,*
https://oceanwide-expeditions.com/blog/how-and-when-did-greenland-become-covered-in-ice#:~:text=Scientists%20studied%20Greenland%20for%20decades,approximately%203%20 million%20years%20ago.

III. Some problems with wind and solar power

As solar and wind generated electricity are the other carbon free power to compete with nuclear power, it is useful to take a dispassionate look at them. There are many constraints based on fundamental science, economics, and environmental matters, which show that they can never be a major source of power, at least not given the present knowledge.

To see immediately how advocacy of solar and wind distorts the truth, most reports on solar and wind apparatus quote the 'nameplate' power. This is the maximum the device generates when conditions are exactly right. But conditions are rarely exactly right. Nameplate power is not the important power, average power is. For instance, a solar panel might produce a kilowatt at high noon on a summer day, but averaging over all conditions, it would be more like 200 Watts. A wind turbine might produce 2 Megawatts (MW) when the wind is blowing at the right speed, from the right direction, but perhaps only 500 Kilowatts (kW) averaged over all condition. In most conventional power stations, coal, gas, nuclear, the average power is very nearly the peak or desired power, so there is little confusion. A 1-Gigawatt electric (billion Watts, GWe) power plant, rarely runs at 150 MW. However, a 1 GWe nameplate power solar voltaic farm runs at zero power for at least half the time. Hence, reports on solar and wind power have a tremendous potential for confusion, as the nameplate power (usually reported) is typically a factor of 4 or 5 times the average power (the more meaningful number). It is important to keep this fact in mind when going over claims of delivered power. Advocates of solar and wind, unfortunately, often talk of nameplate power, as if it were average power.

As we will see, a large transition to solar and wind power, has for the most part caused havoc and economic loss in the places where it plays a major role. It has caused frequent blackouts and greatly rising cost to the consumer, and this is in parts of the world that are the richest and most prosperous parts of the world. Not only that, but it also has no environmental benefit, in fact it is the dirtiest power source existing today. It causes environmental devastation in the places where the large amounts of material necessary for it are mined, in the tremendous amount of land used (really wasted) where the windmills and solar panels are installed, and in the places where its trash is disposed of. The western democracies are engaged in a large-scale attempted transition to wind and solar; the rest of the world is not. Many countries hostile to the values of democracy are only increasing their fossil fuel and nuclear power. This is obviously a concern for national security as well.

When reading all the adoring media on how economic, safe, reliable, and environmentally viable solar panels and wind turbines are, it pays to keep in mind Richard Feynman's famous quote regarding the Challenger disaster: "When introducing a new technology, reality has to take precedence over public relations, for nature cannot be fooled".

As a final indication of the lack of confidence of the world in the potential of solar and wind power, there was a large international meeting to discuss the climate dilemma in Scotland in November 2021. World leaders, including President Biden and many European leaders attended. However, the leaders of Brazil, Russia, China, and Turkey voted with their feet, and did not attend. The leader of India attended but announced that India would not be reducing its CO_2 emission until 2070; realistically, a meaningless commitment. These are large, important, technically advanced countries, containing ~ 40% of the world population. Their unwillingness to participate demonstrates not only their skepticism of the nearly universal western claims of a climate crisis, but also their skepticism of solar and wind power. The western countries are not all that different. Typically, some western bureaucrat says that we must stop or reduce the use of fossil in this way and that. Occasionally the new rule is put to a vote, and the new rule is almost always rejected by the voters. Or as Yogi Berra put it "If people don't want to come to the ballpark, you can't stop 'em"

The solar and wind power available

When considering solar and wind power, the very first issue is what is the available power? Solar power, in mid latitudes, at high noon on a summer day is about 1Gigawatt (GW) per square kilometer. However, averaging over night and day (cutting it in half), solar angle and added absorption from the longer path (cutting it about in half again), sun, rain, snow, clouds…. , it is roughly 200 MW/km². The maximum efficiency of a solar panel is given by the Shockley Queisser (1) limit of ~30%. Most operating solar panels are around 15-20%, so they are near the theoretical maximum. Assuming this 20% efficiency figure, a 1GW solar average power plant would cover about 25 km², and the land could not be used for anything else. While this sounds small compared to the area of, say the United States, Russia, Brazil, or China, it would be difficult to find this amount of land available in say the American northeast. The cost of rural land there is about $5000 per acre, so 25km² would cost ~$25M. This is not that great a deterrent but finding 25 available contiguous square kilometers in a place like the American northeast probably is. The 15-20% efficient solar panels cost ~$3/nameplate Watt, so these would cost ~ $15B for the 1 GW average power solar farm. Then there is the cost of installation and hook up and maintenance. To do this one needs a team of skilled workers, working over every square inch of the 25 km². Likely it dominates the cost of the solar installations.

Let us consider the peak power, average power, and cost of a large solar farm in the United States. Consider the Topaz Solar Farm, in California, a region of the country which one would expect to be very hospitable to solar power, as opposed to for instance the rainy, snowy east coast or midwest [2]. At one time Topaz was the world's larges solar facility. It covered and area of 13 square kilometers, but as Figure 1 shows, it does not cover all of the allowed space. It is billed as having a capacity of 580 MW, but looking at the small print, it delivers 1,200,000 Megawatt hours every year, meaning its average power is 130MW, not much more than one fifth of the advertised power. The cost to build it was $2.5B, or roughly $20B for a 1 GW average power plant. However this published figure is most likely a significant underestimate of the cost, when everything is taken into account. The facility as run into financial trouble, and is considering bankrupcy (3).

Figure 1: An aerial photo of the Topaz solar farm in California. For a while it was the world's largest solar facility. Can this land be used also for anything else? From ref. (2)

Now let us consider wind power. Only about 1-2% of the solar power impingement on earth goes into wind. Generously granting 2%, and considering the Betz limit [4] on the maximum efficiency of the conversion of wind power to mechanical energy of 60%, we assume 50% efficiency. Hence a 1GW average power wind farm would cover at least 500 km^2. Unlike a solar farm, this land could be used for some other purposes, but not many. It could be used for grazing animals, and perhaps for growing some crops not requiring much human intervention, but it is unfit for human habitation. The noise would be very disturbing to many, and in the winter, in the cold regions of the country, large chunks of ice, hundreds of kilograms, fall off the turbine blades, killing anyone that were struck by them. This author took a trip to Quebec over the 2022 Christmas holiday. It was very cold and there was a good bit of snow on the ground. On the roofs of many 3 and 4 story buildings, workers, chained there for their safety, were shoveling ice off the roofs. This falling ice presents a real danger to pedestrians, and many years see one or two killed by it. Imagine the damage a 100 kg chunk of ice, falling off a 500-foot wind turbine would do. At least in the Americannortheast, are 500 km^2 of reasonably contiguous land, without human habitation available anywhere?

The cost of a turbine is typically ~$2/Watt of nameplate power, or ~$8/Watt of average power. If one considers 4 MW nameplate power turbines (about the height of the Washington monument), the 1GW average power plant needs ~1000 at a cost ~$8B. This does not account for the cost of installation, putting up 1000 structures the size of the Washington monument could not be cheap! And how much does 500 km^2 of contiguous land cost, especially in a place like the American northeast or west cost?

It is not only their cost, but these wind turbines are also unsightly, and certainly destroy the scenic and tourist appeal of many areas where they are installed, as Figure 2 demonstrates.

Figure 2: Modern windmills just beyond a small village in Germany. They do not look like they are delivering any power at this point, the blades are not the slightest bit blurry. Does anyone want to go to a B&B or guest house here for a nice relaxing vacation? Does anyone want to take a nice country walk here? How much has the tourist economy lost here?

The (un)reliability of solar power

Recently, under adverse weather conditions, at least 4 places which relied heavily on solar and wind lost power for substantial periods of time. These are not places in poor areas of the world, which struggle to afford minimum power, but in 4 of the richest places in the world, Germany, California, Texas, and Britain.

Texas is usually a warm state, but being in the great plains, every few years it experiences a frigid winter. That was its experience in February 2021, where it was snow covered and frigid (for Texas) for a long period of time. Texas has made a large investment in solar and wind power, one quarter of the wind power of the United States is in Texas. In the winter this failed; see Figure 3. Much of the state experienced long periods without electric power as windmills froze (5) and solar panels became snow covered (6, 7, 8).

Figure 3: Frozen windmills in Texas, February 2021. (5)

With the failure of wind and solar, gas-powered plants rushed in to take up the slack, but were only able to partially fill in, especially with the increased demand due to the weather. Figure 4 is a graph of the power supplied by various power sources in Texas during the week of worst power loss.

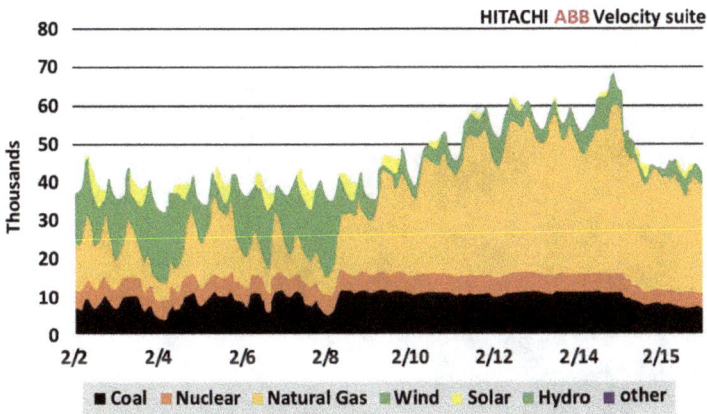

Figure 4: Power delivered to Texas from various sources during 2 weeks in February 2021. Notice the great reduction in wind and solar, and the struggle of gas to keep up.

The Wall Street Journal (5) even mentioned that the Texas problem in the winter was not its only problem. In June 2021, there was a heat spell, certainly not unusual for Texas, and again solar and wind largely failed, with gas rushing to take up as much of the slack as it could.

Search the Texas dilemma on the internet, and everything but their reliance on wind and solar is blamed (more evidence of mass delusion). However Oklahoma had about the same weather as Texas, but did not rely on wind and solar to nearly the same extent, and had no problem.

Germany also has been relying very strongly on wind and solar, and the severe winter of 2020-2021 has played havoc with it. The country was exceptionally cold and snow covered, and large parts of the country lost electric power for a long period of time. Germany attempted to purchase power from neighboring countries, but there was none at any price to sell; they could supply only their own population. Figure 5 shows a snow-covered solar panel in Germany, and its effect

on their school children as they attempted to do their homework (8).

Figure 5: Snow covered solar panels in Germany, and its effect on their school children. (8)

Of course, the Fact Checkers jumped all over these claims, saying that German renewable power worked just fine during the winter. (Did you ever notice that the 'Fact Checkers' never fact check the outrageous claims of the wonders of wind and solar?) However, in this instance, their own graphs belied their claim (9). Figure 6, redrawn from (9) so as to be more visible, shows their graph of the various components of German power from mid-January to mid-February 2021. Clearly it demonstrates that from January 24-29, January 31-February 3, and February 9-17 solar and wind basically quit, and conventional power systems made up the shortage as best they could. But what happens when Germany turns exclusively to solar and wind?

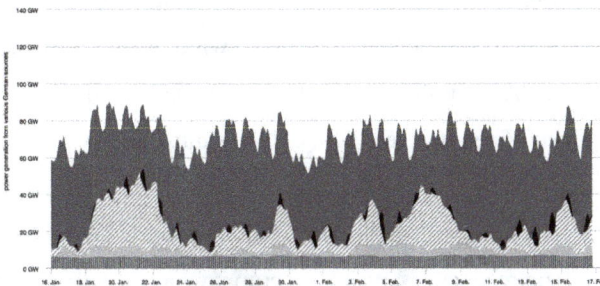

Figure 6: A redrawn graph from the 'Fact Checkers' on German power from Mid January to Mid February, showing that Solar and wind basically quit for nearly half of this time. The top graph in medium grey is the power delivered by conventional sources, mostly coal; the light graph with the diagonal lines is the land based wind power delivered, the dark splotches atop that is the solar power, the light grey graph near the bottom is the sea based wind power, and the dark graph on the bottom with the vertical lines is the biofuel power plus the hydro power. Redrawn from (9)

California has been converting to solar power over the last decade or two. It had decommissioned all of its coal fired power plants, and its nuclear power plants except for Diablo Canyon. It has some gas fired power but minimizes it to the extent possible. The state had a great deal of solar power available on summer afternoons, but this faded away in the late afternoon and evening when air condition was most needed. In a heat wave in summer 2021, it did not have enough power, and had to instigate rolling blackouts (5). It attempted to purchase power from other states, but it already gets about 1/3 of its power from neighboring states, and none was available.

The Wall Street Journal ended their editorial (5) with the sentence: "Pro survival tip: Buy a diesel generator – while you still can."

Solar power from photovoltaic sources can only be used when the sun is shining; wind power, only when the wind is blowing. Thus, to have reliable power, solar and wind power must be backed up by another power source which runs under all conditions. Gas-powered plants are used for this purpose. This is not an unreasonable approach, but of course to evaluate the total cost, that of the gas plants, often idle, must be added to the cost to wind or solar. As the Wall Street Journal phrased it "A big problem is that subsidies and mandates have spurred an over-development of renewables, which has resulted in gas plants operating at lower levels or even idle much of the time. Keeping standby units in top condition is hugely expensive. So, when plants are required to run all out to meet surging demand or back up renewables, problems crop up – as they did this week." (5)

To provide backup power, there is talk of a revolution in battery technology, but this seems far-fetched. The Tesla car's lithium-ion battery stores about 100 kwhrs. The United States uses 400 gigawatts (GW) of electric power, and if one section of the country is out of wind or sunshine, say Texas or California, the battery backup would have to provide this power, probably ~ 100 GW. The Tesla battery would provide this backup for 3.6 microseconds! We would need ~3×10^5 batteries to provide a second's worth, ~ twenty-four billion to provide a day; ~100 Billion for four days, and this is probably not sufficient. The United States would need probably half a dozen to a dozen of these battery stations across the country. A Tesla battery now costs around \$5-10k. Even assuming the cost could be reduced to \$1000, the cost of the backup system for the United States for four days would be ~ \$600 trillion. It makes no sense!

Of course, any energy storage scheme, which stores that much energy, will represent a potential danger. However, the danger involved in storing it in lithium-ion batteries is unique. The batteries have a well-known fire danger, even when the battery is not delivering power. Furthermore, once the fire starts, it is very difficult to extinguish with conventional fire suppression techniques. For instance, there was a fire at the Tesla battery factory near Monterey California in September 2022 (10) which was difficult to put out. Nearby residents were told not to venture outside, and to keep their doors and windows closed. The 100 billion batteries in each battery stations have a stored energy of roughly equivalent to that of a ten-megaton bomb.

The danger is particularly acute on an airplane, where fires in the hold have occurred, occasionally bringing down a plane when flying at altitude. While these were cargo planes with no passengers, the crew was killed from Lithium battery fires in Boeing 747 flights over both South Korea and Dubai in 2010 and 2011 (11). Figure 6 illustrates the potential danger to the aircraft.

Figure 6: A UPS large freight aircraft destroyed (fortunately on the ground) from a fire of lithium batteries in the hold. (11)

It is not only cargo planes that had to deal with fire. China Southern Airlines, Flight CZ3539 had a fire in the overhead luggage bin (12). Fortunately, it was when the plane was boarding, and not when it was in the air, and everyone could disembark with no injuries. If that fire had ignited an hour later, who knows what catastrophe might have occurred. Figure 7 is a photo taken on the plane.

Figure 7: Luckily for these passengers, the plane had not yet taken off. (12)

It is not only aircraft that are vulnerable. Hamden CT, possibly in an example of virtue signaling, said that it would transition much of its bus fleet to electric buses (13). In July 2022 one caught fire while not being used, but was simply parked. Figure (8) is a photo of the burning bus. There have been many stories of electric bus fires all over the world.

Figure 8 The Li ion battery in this bus in Hamden CT caught fire in July 2022, while the bus was parked. (13)

When buses are parked in bus terminals, the danger is even more acute, as the fire can rapidly spread from one bus to another (14) as was experienced in China recently.   Figure (9) is a photo of a fire starting in one parked bus, and rapidly spreading to three others.

Figure 9: The Li Ion battery fire started in the bus on the right, and quickly spread to 3 of the 4 buses parked nearby. (14)

The material requirements for solar and wind

Sunlight and wind may be free, but the infrastructure to convert these into usable electric power, and the material needed are very considerable (15). This has been studied by the Manhattan Institute by Mark Mills. As an example, Figure 10, from Ref (16) shows a schematic of the number of different materials required to construct different types of power plants, per terawatt hour. Clearly a 1 GW wind farm, will use about ten times the material as a gas-powered plant, and a 1 GW solar panel farm, nearly 20 times as much.

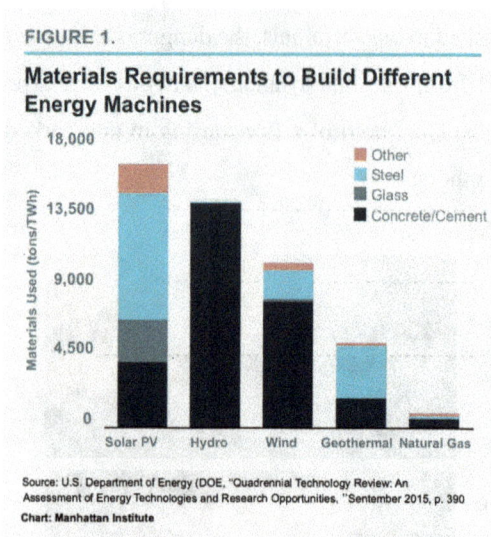

FIGURE 1.

Materials Requirements to Build Different Energy Machines

Materials Used (tons/TWh)

- Other
- Steel
- Glass
- Concrete/Cement

Solar PV   Hydro   Wind   Geothermal   Natural Gas

Source: U.S. Department of Energy (DOE, "Quadrennial Technology Review: An Assessment of Energy Technologies and Research Opportunities, "Sentember 2015, p. 390

Chart: Manhattan Institute

Figure 10: The material needed for solar, hydro, wind, geothermal, and natural gas plants. Clearly the wind and solar use tremendously more materials of all kinds, than do gas fired plants. (16)

An important element for manufacturing modern batteries is lithium. It is usually found in high desert areas, and mining it is extremely water intensive. For instance, one of the best sources of lithium in the United States is in Death Valley. Mining lithium in these areas typically needs about 2 metric tons of water for each kilogram of lithium extracted. A typical Tesla battery typically has about 10 kg of lithium, requiring the use of 20 metric tons of water (17, 18). The hundred billion or so Tesla batteries required to provide backup power for the United States, say every ten years, would more than double the country's water infrastructure, and do so in some of the country's driest places. This water demand, in addition that of the cost, is another reason 'it makes no sense'.

The cost for delivered power

It is often claimed that solar and wind electrical energy is getting cheaper, and often much cheaper than that of generated by coal, gas, oil or nuclear, for instance (19). While these have no fuel costs, as we have seen in the last section, the material and labor costs, compared to conventional power costs are enormous. After all the labor cost of installing a 1 GW average power wind farm, namely ~1000 modern 4GW name plate power turbines, each as tall as the Washington Monument, over an area of at least 500 square kilometers, must be quite high compared to installing a single building housing a 1 GW gas powered plant.

Hence, there are enormous scientific, technical, economic, and environmental, barriers which are in reality, just about impossible to overcome (20,21). Furthermore, there are government subsidies in most countries which affect the price. These subsidies are very confusing to unravel, but likely, they are significant (22).

The skeptical arguments, while correct, are not necessarily easy for a layman to follow. After all who, in say the United States, notices or cares if, to build solar panels and wind turbines, we must dig up a lot of indium, lanthanum, neodymium, europium and other rare earth elements somewhere, likely in some remote, poor African country, which will not complain about us trashing its environment, due to its necessarily weak mining safety and environmental laws and paying its citizens slave wages.

It is now possible to compare nuclear to solar and wind on a large scale. There is what this author has called 'a gigantic laboratory' in Europe (23). It is France and Germany. France for years has generated most of its electricity (~75-80%) by nuclear power. Germany, in about 2000, had adopted a different route. It has embarked on an 'energiewende', a German word for energy transformation to solar and wind energy. Accordingly, it has decommissioned many of its coal fired power plants and is in the process of decommissioning what once were its 17 nuclear power reactors. At this point, it is getting about 25-30% of its electrical power from wind and/or solar; the rest from other sources. Some articles on the energiewende, call it a smashing success (24, mass delusion) ; others, a dismal failure (25).

Where does the truth lie?

There is one thing anybody can easily figure out. Namely despite all the claims of low cost solar and wind, how does the cost of electricity in Germany and France compare? This is simple and noncontroversial. Furthermore, since the whole purpose of the energiewende is to reduce the CO_2 input into the atmosphere, how well do Germany and France do? Again, this is simple and noncontroversial. Figure 11 shows a graph of the price of a kilowatt hour of electric energy in Germany, France and the United States, in euro cents, from 1980 to about 2020 (26, 23, and other sources). Also shown on the graph are plots of per capita CO_2 emission into the atmosphere in tons per year (27,23 and other sources).

USA -- Green
Germany -- Red
France -- Blue

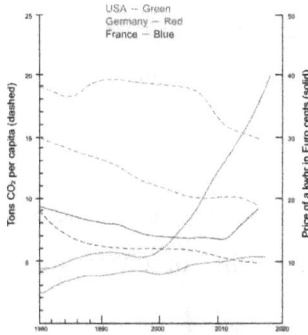

Figure 11: Plot of the cost of a kilowatt hour of electric energy in euro cents in France, Germany and the USA (solid), and emission of CO_2 into the atmosphere in tons per capita per year. (23,26,27)

The graph shows that, at least up to now, after ~20 years, the German energiewende has failed on both counts. It has not reduced the price of electricity, but rather has greatly increased it. It has not reduced the per capita German CO_2 emission into the atmosphere as compared to France, or even the United States. The impact of the high cost of electricity in Germany is such that almost five million people there were unable to pay their electric bills in 2019, and were cut off from the grid (28).

In summary, France has cheaper electricity and emits less CO2 per capita — both by about half — than does Germany. For those who say that nuclear power is too expensive and environmentally unviable, there is a simple one-word answer, France. The French have had a nuclear economy for decades, and have achieved this economically, without harming any of its citizens, or ruining their environment.

In the last 2 years, as western countries are taking the energy transition more seriously and installing more and more solar and wind power, energy prices are increasing rapidly. Britain has seen a roughly 80% increase in natural gas costs this in 2022 (29), and the United States, after roughly constant, or even decreasing prices for natural gas from 2017 to 2021 (average household winter gas expenditure <$600), has seen a more than 50% jump to the latest estimate for the winter of 2022-23 (average price over $900) (30,31). While much of the media blames everything except:

1. the transition to solar and wind (mass delusion?)
2. the simultaneous canceling of oil leases and pipelines (more mass delusion?),
3. the dismantling of gas and coal fired power plants (still more?),

whom do you believe, the delusional media, or what you see with your own eyes (and feel in your own wallets)?

The conclusion is obvious. Sunlight and wind are free, but converting them to reliable electricity, is very, very expensive.

The end of the life cycle

There is an additional cost and environmental damage of solar and wind power, which has hardly appeared yet. Namely solar panels and wind turbines are only expected to last ~25 years. Since most solar wind panels and wind turbines are younger than this, we have only an inkling of the problem that is rapidly approaching.

Let us first consider solar panels. These panels last about 25 years, so the 250,000 tons we have to dispose of this year is just a trickle compared to the deluge coming at us in 2050, when there will have been a total of 78 million tons to dispose of (i.e 2.5 million per year). These are not appropriate for landfills, as they contain hazardous and poison materials such as lead and cadmium, which can leech into the soil and water supply. However, recycling is expensive. The cost of the recycled materials is considerably more than the cost of the raw materials. For this reason, many places, including (surprisingly!) even environmentally conscious California, are disposing worn out panels in landfills, which is cheap, but environmentally very harmful (32). There are also American efforts to export worn out solar panels to landfills in underdeveloped countries, most likely in Africa. Trashing their environment by taking advantage of their poverty and loose mining restrictions is not enough, we will a trash it even more by sending them our own dangerous garbage, which we cannot safely dispose of in our own country (32). Talk of the moral imperative for the conversion to solar and wind! Even if we had perfect recycling of used solar panels, there is still the environmental danger of their destruction by natural events. A tornado destroyed a solar farm in Southern California, and Hurricane Maria destroyed large solar facilities in Puerto Rico and the Virgin Islands (33). Who knows what damage was done to the local environments? Figure 12 is a photo of a St. Thomas facility after the Hurricane.

Figure 12: A photo of the St. Thomas solar facility after Hurricane Maria

Regarding wind turbines, the problem is twofold. Since the blades are fiber glass and last only about 10 years, we have had considerable experience here. These blades are gigantic, and are very costly to ship and dispose of, but a land fill is a reasonable option if it is large enough. Once they are buried, they will do little if any harm to the local environment. There are just a few landfills in the United States capable of handling these blades. One is near Casper Wyoming. Figure 13 is a photo of a portion of this landfill (34).

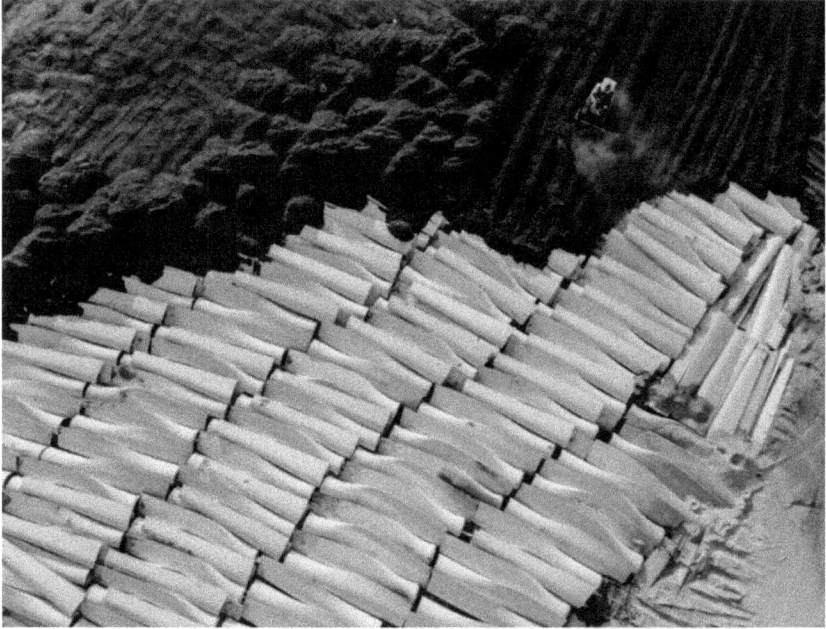

Figure 13: Photograph of fragments of wind turbine blades at their ultimate resting place in a landfill near Casper Wyoming. The small feature in the upper right is a bulldozer driven by a landfill employee. (34)

The difficulty of disposing the blades pales in comparison with disposing of the towers, which last ~25 years. Companies typically must put up decommissioning costs at the outset. The typical cost is apparently $100,000, but this sounds incredibly cheap for dismantling a steel tower the height of the Washington monument. In fact, the Washington Times estimates that a better cost estimate is $500,000 (35) but even that sounds cheap to this author.

The alternative is to walk away and leave them for someone else to worry about. As Tom Lehrer sang in his song about Werner von Braun:

Once rockets go up, who cares where they come down,

That's not my department says Werner von Braun.

Perhaps the wind power providers think that properly disassembling aging turbines is 'not their department'. They are too busy saving the world. There are dueling web pages on this, one saying that there are 14,000 abandoned wind turbines littering the United States (36). Another denies this (37). However, there are certainly many thousand abandoned wind turbines. There are documented to be 1600 in Altamont pass in California alone in 2014 (38). The internet mentions other abandoned wind farms in California, Texas (39), Hawaii (40), Oklahoma (41) and Wyoming.

Figure 14 are photos of abandoned wind turbines in California, Texas, Hawaii and Oklahoma.

Altamont Pass, California 2014 (38)

Near Harlingen, Texas 2017 (39)

Oahu's north shore, Hawaii 2012 (40)

Oklahoma pan handle, July 2021   (41)

Figure 14: Abandoned wind turbines in the United States

Of course, there is talk of recycling the wind turbines once they have outlived their usefulness. Perhaps some, but certainly not all the take down cost can be recovered. However, one thing that cannot be recovered, at any reasonable cost, is the 500 ton steel and concrete base (42) . These will litter the landscape forever. Figure 15 is a photo of such a base.

Figure 15, a photo of the 500 ton steel and concrete base of a wind turbine. (42)

Five hundred years from now, our descendants will wander around places like this and ask each other what the heck are these monsters that their primitive ancestors constructed, and why are there so many of them?

Considering the enormous amount of land and material they need, at their birth, solar and wind installations, do great harm to the overall environment where the material is mined, in areas with loose mining restrictions (i.e Western China, Africa…). As they are used, they take up an enormous amount of land which can be much more useful for other, more standard uses, i.e. housing, industry, conservation, crops, tourism, animal grazing…. At their death, they are even more harmful, where do you put their remnants? They almost certainly form more of an environmental crisis than any other power source.

Subsidies and total cost for the transition to decarbonize

There are many conflicting elements of this cost, including government subsidies, which are difficult (perhaps deliberately) to unravel. The Washington Times (35) estimates the US government subsidies for constructing wind turbines between 2016 and 2020 was ~$24B.

Other estimates for the American subsidies are even higher. For instance, the Government pays $7500 toward the cost of an American made electric car. Since there are now ~2.3 million of these vehicles in the US, the total subsidy could be as high as $17B, going only to the very richest and (mistakenly) most environmentally conscious car buyers.

Recent legislation has government sponsored support for 'green energy' at $300B for the next decade, or ~ $30B per year:

"The legislation earmarks more than $100 billion over the next decade for renewables such as wind and solar, amounting to roughly a third of the $300 billion in clean energy spending called for in the bill's green energy subtitle." (43)

While there is confusion (likely deliberate) on the dollars, euros, yen… going to subsidize wind and solar energy, there is one thing that all proponents of the transition seem to agree on. The total worldwide yearly cost for the transition is in the neighborhood of at least half a trillion dollars. Yet these authorities point out that this is only about 10-15% of what is needed to make the transition, namely $4-6T per year for the next 30 years. Total cost for the transition is estimated at between $150T (44) to $275T (45). Actually, this author believes the transition is impossible at any price, and will be a colossal waste of money and resources. However, for the purpose of this analysis, we assume a total cost for the transition of ~$250T.

To summarize, the false assumption of a climate crisis, is causing a real energy crisis in the west. All this as the less developed parts of the world are greatly increasing their coal consumption. Based on the incorrect assumption of such a rapidly oncoming climate crisis, constantly backed up by propaganda from both those who expect to profit from it, and those who mistakenly think they are aiding the environment, we are advised to waste ~$250T over the next generation or so. All of this for a new system that ignores a perfectly reasonable approach for attaining future sustainable power, while maintaining modern civilization. Instead it proposes a system that will not work, and will destroy modern civilization, due to its failure to provide economical, reliable and environmentally viable power. However many countries, basically hostile to the west want nothing to do with this. As we destroy our economies and impoverish our people, especially the poorer among us, these other countries will surge as they add conventional power. Wasting resources on this scale, a scale large enough to destroy a civilization, is nearly unprecidented in human history. The French building the palace at Versailles, while the English were using their resources to build ships, pales by comparason. Perhaps the ancient Egyptians construction of the pyramids was comparable. Who knows what the result would have been if instead, the Egyptians had used these resources to build an ocean going merchant marine and navy, the knowledge to do so existed at the time. If the west keeps going on this path, there will be not only an energy crisis, but a national security crisis as well.

For all the publicity and propaganda on how cheap solar power is, its *proponents* estimate of the cost range from $100 trillion, to $275 trillion by 2050, to decarbonize the world's energy systems (44,45). But we have just seen that it costs at least this to provide backup lithium-ion battery power in a single country, the United States.

The fact that these enormous figures seem to be simply accepted by the public and media, seems to this author to be proof of a mass delusion. After all, this is our money, and a tremendous amount of it! Why is nobody asking questions like 'Do we really need this?', 'How much will I have to pay?' 'Just exactly what do we get for it.' 'Does it really save the planet?' 'What do the opponents of this say? 'What do the thousands of scientists who oppose this say?' "Why are they being canceled all over social media?' 'If a temperature rise of ~1.5o C from the preindustrial value will produce catastrophe, how come the temperature rise we have already experienced of ~1.1o C has produced only benefit?' 'Are there better things we can spend $275T on?' Are we being like sheep marching calmly to the slaughter? Lemmings running to the cliff?

To plagiarize from Lindzen:

"What historians will definitely wonder about in future centuries is how flawed logic, obscured by shrewd and unrelenting propaganda from those who stand to profit, actually enabled a coalition of powerful special interests to convince nearly everyone that the world's power infrastructure, which basically works, must be replaced with another which will fail, and along the way will destroy modern civilization. It will be remembered not only as the greatest mass delusion, but also as the greatest con in the history of the world- that snake oil salesmen at one time convinced the world to spend ~$275T to throw out its working power system and replace it with a harebrained Rube Goldberg gadget".

References

1. William Shockley, and Hans J. Queisser, *Detailed balance limit of efficiency of p-n junction solar cells,* Journal of Applied Physics. 1961 **32** 510–519. Also see *Shockley-Queisser limit*, wikipedia, https://en.wikipedia.org/wiki/Shockley%E2%80%93Queisser_limit

2. Topaz solar, https://en.wikipedia.org/wiki/Topaz_Solar_Farm

3. Leslie, Kaytlyn, *Carrizo Plaines solar farm's credid rating drops to 'junk' as PG&E bankruptcy looms,* The Tribune, San Luis Obispo, January, 17, 2019 https://www.sanluisobispo.com/news/local/article224632960.html

4. *Betz limit,* wikipedia https://en.wikipedia.org/wiki/Betz%27s_law

5. *California and Texas Greenouts,* WSJ Editorial, June 17, 2021 /

6. H. Sterling Burnett**,** Pro/Con: *Green energy was the main cause of Texas' deep freeze,* Duluth News Tribune, March 1, 2021

7. Kent Knutson, *Great Winter Storm of 2021 Will Live in Grid History,* Power Magazine, Feb 19, 2021, https://www.powermag.com/great-winter-storm-of-2021-will-live-in-grid-history/

8. Lori Foti, *Germany's 'Green' Energy Failure: Germany turns back to coal and natural gas as millions of its solar panels are blanketed in snow and ice,* World News ERA, February 11, 2021

9. Sarah Schmidt Fact Check: Germany's Wind Turbines And Solar Panels Did NOT Suddenly Stop Working Due To Weather Conditions
Fact Check   Feb 17, 2021
https://leadstories.com/hoax-alert/2021/02/fact-check-germanys-wind-turbines-and-solar-panels-did-not-suddenly-stop-working-due-to-weather-conditions.html

10. California's Tesla Battery Fire, Wall Streed Journal WSJ Sept 21, 2022 https://www.wsj.com/articles1californias-tesla-battery-fire-monterey-green-energy-fossil-fuels-11663796046?mod=opinion_lead_pos3

11. Abigail Brone, NTSB joins probe of CT's 'rare' electric bus fire; only 18 verified incidents globally since 2010, CT Insider Aug 1m 2022

https://www.ctinsider.com/hartford/article/NTSB-joins-probe-of-CT-s-rare-electric-17340231.php

12. Bibby, Neil, *Lithium ion battery fire in an aircraft overhead luggage bin,* Asia Pacific Fire News, February 26, 2018
https://apfmag.mdmpublishing.com/lithium-ion-battery-fire-in-an-aircraft-overhead-luggage-bin/

13. Abigail Brone, NTSB joins probe of CT's 'rare' electric bus fire; only 18 verified incidents globally since 2010, CT Insider Aug 1m 2022
https://www.ctinsider.com/hartford/article/NTSB-joins-probe-of-CT-s-rare-electric-17340231.php

14. Linda, Electric Bus Battery explosion fires, Gridedge Storage News, May 27, 2022, https://gridedgenews.com/electric-bus-battery-explosion-fires/

15. Lars Schernikau, William Smith, and Rosemary Falcon, Full cost of electricity 'FCOE' and energy returns 'eROI', Journal of Management and Sustainability; Vol. 12, 2022, No. 1; 2022 ISSN 1925-4725
https://papers.ssrn.com/sol3/papers.cfm?abstract_id=4000800
16. Mills, Mark, *Mines, Materials, and "Green" Energy, a Reality Check*, Manhattan Institute Report, July 2020.
https://media4.manhattan-institute.org/sites/default/files/mines-minerals-green-energy-reality-checkMM.pdf
17. Hooke, Alexander, *Lithium batteries, another false panacea for eliminating fossil fuels,* Washington Times, September 29, 2021
18. Scarlett Evans, *Lithium's water problem, Mining Technology,* January 27, 2021
By Scarlett Evans27 Jan 2021 (Last Updated July 19th, 2021 08:55)
https://www.mining-technology.com/features/lithiums-water-problem/
19.John Timmer, *Wind power prices now lower than the cost of natural gas*, ARS Technia, August 17, 2019
https://arstechnica.com/science/2019/08/wind-power-prices-now-lower-than-the-cost-of-natural-gas/
20. Shellenberger, Michael, *Apocalypse never, why environmental alarmism hurts us all,* , Harper Collins, 2020
21. Mills, Mark, *The new energy economy, and exercise in magical thinking*, Manhattan Institute Report, March 26, 2019
https://www.manhattan-institute.org/green-energy-revolution-near-impossible
22. David Keene, *The trouble with wind farms*, Washington Times, Jan 1, 2020

23. Wallace Manheimer, *Midcentury carbon free sustainable energy development based on fusion breeding*, IEEE Access, December 2018, Vol 6, issue 1, p 64954-64969, https://ieeexplore.ieee.org/document/8502757

24. John Mathews, *The spectacular success of the German 'energiewende' and what needs to be done next*, The energy post. EU, October 10, 2017, https://energypost.eu/the-spectacular-success-of-the-german-energiewende-and-what-needs-to-be-done-next/
25. Frank Dohman, Alexander Jung, Stefan Schultz and Gerald Traufetter, *German Failure on the Road to a Renewable Future* , Der Spiegel, May 13, 2019
26. Subsidized wind, *Subsidized Wind & Solar Set to Quadruple German Power Prices*, Stop these things, March 17, 2017

https://stopthesethings.com/2017/03/17/subsidised-wind-solar-set-to-quadruple-german-power-prices/
27. *Cumultive Effects Under UNFCCC*, On climate change policy, November 26, 2018, https://onclimatechangepolicydotorg.wordpress.com/2018/11/26/cumulative-emissions-under-the-unfccc/

28. Editorial team, *More and more Germans cannot pay for their electricity*, Die Freie Welt, April 3, 2019
29. Households across the U.K. are about to experience an 80% jump in energy costs, NPR, August 26, 2022

https://www.npr.org/2022/08/26/1119567595/households-across-the-u-k-are-about-experience-an-80-jump-in-energy-costs
30. Get ready for the big Chill, Wall Street Journal editorial, Oct 18, 2022
https://www.wsj.com/articles/get-ready-for-the-big-chill-energy-prices-heating-fuel-energy-information-administration-11666121518?mod=opinion_lead_pos3

31. US natural gas bills will increase in all regions this winter, Today in Energy, EIA, October 17, 2022, https://www.eia.gov/todayinenergy/detail.php?id=54259&utm_source=substack&utm_mediu m=email

32. Solar panels, *Solar Panels Are Starting to Die, Leaving Behind Toxic Trash*, Wired, August 22, 2020
https://www.wired.com/story/solar-panels-are-starting-to-die-leaving-behind-toxic-trash/

33. Shellenberger, Michael, *If Solar Panels Are So Clean, Why Do They Produce So Much Toxic Waste?*, Forbes, May 23, 2018

https://www.forbes.com/sites/michaelshellenberger/2018/05/23/if-solar-panels-are-so-clean-why-do-they-produce-so-much-toxic-waste/?sh=35c43606121c

34. Martin, Chris, *Wind Turbine Blades Can't Be Recycled, So They're Piling Up in Landfills*, Bloomberg Green, February 7, 2020

35. Keene, David, *The trouble with wind farms*, Washington Times, Jan 1, 2020

36. Abandoned wind, https://www.riteon.org.au/14000-abandoned-wind-turbines-litter-the-united-states/

37. Fact check,
https://www.politifact.com/factchecks/2019/oct/25/chain-email/no-there-arent-14000-abandoned-wind-turbines-litte/

38. Molly Lautamo, Altamon pass*: What's the story with those windmills*,
Santa Cruz Waves, November 19, 2014
https://www.santacruzwaves.com/2014/11/altamont-pass-whats-the-story-with-those-windmills/

39. Kelley, Rick, *Retiring worn-out wind turbines could cost billions that nobody has*, Valley Morning Star (Harlingen TX), February 21, 2017
https://energycentral.com/news/retiring-worn-out-wind-turbines-could-cost-billions-nobody-has

40. Leonard, Tom, *Broken down and rusting, is this the future of Britain's 'wind rush'?* Daily Mail (British newspaper), 18 March 2012

41. AP News, July 25, 2021,
https://apnews.com/article/business-604e607e4e267e21399dab3a49d80200/gallery/a440427e993347e28b89ff3ab965c7d9

42. Permanent Legacy: Wind Industry Plans to Abandon Millions of 500 Tons of Concrete Wind Turbine Bases, Stop these things October 13, 2021

https://stopthesethings.com/2021/10/13/permanent-legacy-wind-industry-plans-to-abandon-millions-of-500-tonne-concrete-wind-turbine-bases/

43. Benjamin Storrow, Congress poised to dramatically alter clean energy subsidies, E&E News Climate wire, 11/16/2021
https://www.eenews.net/articles/congress-poised-to-dramatically-alter-clean-energy-subsidies/

44. , Barbara Ruchner, Axel Clark, Angela Falconer et al, *Global Landscape of Climate Finance, 2019* Climate Policy Initiative, November 7, 2019
https://www.climatepolicyinitiative.org/publication/global-landscape-of-climate-finance-2019/

45. Vaclav Simil, Numbers don't lie, IEEE Spectrum, p22, October 2022 His figure is $275T to decarbonize the economy by 2050

IV. Fusion

As fusion is a relatively small R&D project, at least compared to the trillions going into the climate effort, most of the world has only vague knowledge of it. Hence there is no such thing as a mass delusion in the fusion world, i.e. there is no 'mass'. However not only can the development of fusion be affected by mass delusions in other parts of the world, but portions of the fusion effort can also be affected by the 'cancel culture' which prevails when there is a mass delusion.

The fusion reactions

The world has been attempting to develop economical fusion reactors for more than half a century. While great progress has been made, there still is a very long way to go. In a fusion reaction, two isotopes of hydrogen, deuterium and tritium join to form a helium nucleus, and in the process release an energetic neutron and an energetic alpha particle (i.e. a helium nucleus). Note that while deuterium occurs in nature, tritium does not. It must be bred from a reaction of a lithium nucleus with a neutron. The energy of these fusion particles would be absorbed by some sort of heat exchanger, called a blanket, and this would generate electric power in the standard way. It is regarded as a clean energy system, one which produces no by product which is either a proliferation risk or a pollutant. A schematic of this reaction is shown in Figure (1).

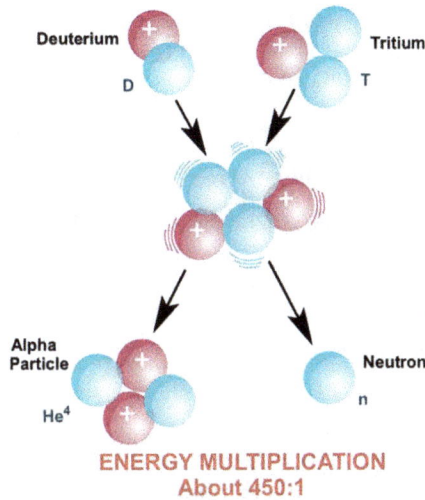

Deuterium
D

Tritium
T

Alpha
Particle

Neutron

He^4

n

ENERGY MULTIPLICATION
About 450:1

Figure 1: schematic of the fusion DT reaction. To overcome the Coulomb barrier and react, the positively charged D and T must have energy about 10 kiloelectron volts (keV) or more (atoms burning in a typical fire have energy of about 0.1 electron Volt). The fusion products are a 14 Million electron Volt (MeV) neutron, and a 3.5 MeV alpha particle (i.e. a helium nucleus). In a conventional fission reactor, the neutrons that form the chain reaction are produced at ~ 2MeV, and the fission fragments are produced at ~ 200 MeV. Hence the fusion reaction produces much more energetic neutrons than a fission reaction reactor. However, it takes 10 fusion reactions to produce the energy of one fission reaction. Both facts, as we will see, are the key to the great advantage of fusion breeding over fission breeding.

A problem is that to form this reaction, the energy of the D and T are so high that they cannot be part of a liquid or solid, but rather form a fully ionized gas called a plasma. The fusion plasma consists of deuterium and tritium ions, and free electrons. This plasma is so hot that it cannot be in contact with any material surface. Hence in the fusion effort, the plasma would be confined by magnetic fields, and the process is thereby called magnetic fusion energy (MFE), or by its own inertia, and the process is called inertial fusion energy (IFE).

To orient ourselves, we now list the most common possible fusion reactions. The most important of these is the DT reaction, it has the highest reaction rate and requires the minimum plasma temperature.

D+T→→n(14.1MeV)+He(3.5MeV)

The deuterium for this reaction can easily be supplied by the world's oceans and the amount is basically unlimited. About 1/6000 hydrogen atoms is deuterium. A similar reaction uses helium 3 instead of tritium, but because of the additional Coulomb repulsion, requires higher plasma temperature and has a lower reaction rate.

D+^{3}He→→p(14.7MeV)+He(3.6MeV)

One problem with of each of these reactions is that neither tritium nor helium 3 (in usable quantities) exists on earth. Tritium must be bred, and helium 3 exists on the surface of the moon. The fusion project is currently considering only breeding tritium. Tritium can be bred from lithium, and there are two possible breeding reactions. The first is exothermic:

n+6Li→→T(2.75MeV)+He(2.05MeV)

The second possible reaction is endothermic, taking 2.47 MeV away from the reacting particles:

n+7Li→→T+He+n

Clearly this reaction requires an energetic neutron. However, depending on the breeding blanket and the end use, it may be worth the energy price to price to preserve the extra neutron.

A reaction not requiring any breeding is the DD reaction, which may proceed along one of two paths with equal probability for each.

D+D→→n(2.5MeV)+3He(0.8MeV) or

D+D→→p(3MeV)+T(1MeV)

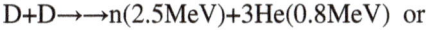

This reaction produces less energy and requires still higher plasma temperature. However, if one looks at it not as a reaction to produce energy, but to breed tritium and helium 3, it could be a viable reaction path, but only after the DT reaction is fully developed.

In Figure 2 are shown reaction rates for the three fusion reactions.

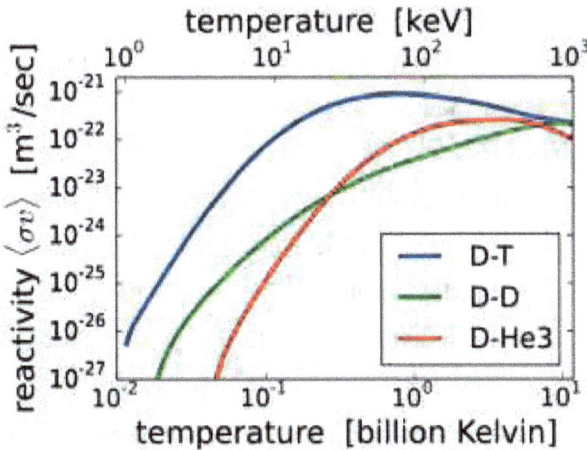

1.

Figure 2. Fusion rate for the three fusion reactions.

Clearly the DT reaction rate is largest and requires the lowest plasma temperature to proceed. The reaction rate maximizes at a temperature about 50 keV. However, the total reaction per unit volume goes as $n^2<\sigma v>$. If the pressure is constrained to some certain value, i.e the density is this pressure divided by the temperature, then the reactions maximize at the temperature where

$<\sigma v>/T^2$ maximizes, or at about 16–17 keV, where the reaction rate is about $<\sigma v>$ $\sim 3 \times 10^{-22}\,\mathrm{m^3/s}$.

We now divide this section into two subsections, one on Magnetic fusion, the other on Inertial (i.e. laser) fusion

Magnetic fusion:

The triple fusion product

An important measure of the capability of any magnetic fusion device is the triple fusion product product $nT\tau$, where n is the density in $\mathrm{m^{-3}}$, T is the temperature in keV, and τ is the energy confinement time in seconds. At fusion temperatures, the DT fusion reaction rate $<\sigma v>$, is roughly proportional to the ion temperature squared. For instance, at 10keV, $<\sigma v> = 1.19 \times 10^{-22}\,\mathrm{m^3/s}$, while at 20 keV, it is, 4.29×10^{-22}. Since the fusion power per unit volume is $n_{DN}n_T W<\sigma v>$, where the n's are the deuteron and triton number density, and W is the fusion energy per reaction, 14 MeV for the neutron and 3.5 for the alpha particle, this power density is roughly proportional to n^2T^2.

However the input power density is simply nT/τ, so the ratio of fusion power to input power, the Q of the device is roughly proportional to $nT\tau$. Table1 enumerates the triple fusion product of a number of magnetic fusion devices. The largest value is 1.6×10^{21}, by the Japanese tokamak JT-60. For a stellarator, the largest value up to now is from the Wendelstein stellarator and is 5×10^{19}. Every other fusion device has a triple fusion product at least two and a half, and even as much as 5 orders of magnitude below what JT-60 has achieved.

Device	nTτ (m⁻³keVsec)	Confined energy (MJ)
Tokamak JT-60	1.6×10^{21}	8.6
Stellarator LHD, Wendelstein*	5×10^{19} *	1.4
ST (NSTX)	5×10^{18}	0.15
RFO (Padua)	3×10^{17}	0.006
Mirror (gas dynamic trap)	1.2×10^{17}	0.03
TAE (field reversed configuration)	6×10^{16}	0.01

Table 1. The triple fusion produce and confined plasma energy for a variety of confinement devices. The asterisk refers to data from Wendelstein, no asterisk refers to data from the Japanese stellarator LHD. The confined energy is in Megajoules (MJ)

Figure 3 shows the rate at which the triple fusion product has advanced for tokamaks, currently the optimum configuration. Note that as the tokamak performance increased rapidly, it was roughly the same as the Moore's law for the performance of computer chips. However, at around 2000, the tokamak performance increased stopped due to the need for much larger, more expensive tokamaks to continue the trend. There has basically no increase in nTτ for more than 20 years.

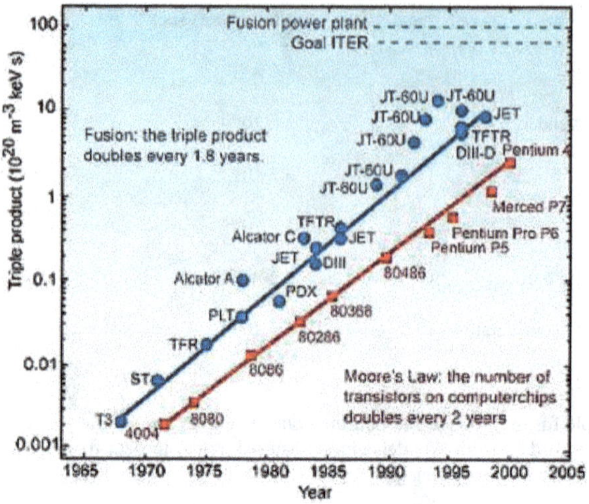

Figure 3. The development of the triple fusion product for tokamaks over the years and for a variety of tokamak devices. The total support for the tokamaks over the years, worldwide, have easily been in the many tens of billions of dollars.

It seems very unlikely that any of the other devices mentioned could catch up to the tokamak in any reasonable time. The tokamaks were designed and built by a large, international coalition, by the best designers and builders of fusion devices at the time. The total effort cost tens of billions of dollars over the 50 or so years of development. Even if these other devices could maintain the same rate of advance, it would take the stellarator (tokamak's closest competitor) more than a decade to catch up with the tokamak, and the field reversed configuration, about 30 years! Who can say for sure that these other configurations will not eclipse the tokamak? However, based on experience up to now, they will not, especially where many of these other configurations have been carefully considered, but rejected, by the major labs or their sponsors. At least as fusion is funded now, there is little likelihood that funds will be made available to spend billions on other devices, i.e. what is needed to catch up to tokamaks assuming they can catch up at all. This is certainly true at least until the large tokamaks now under construction can show what they can do. Realistically, at least for the next decade or so, the tokamak is the only game in town.

The triple product for JT-60 is based on confining a plasma with a density of about 10^{20} m^{-3}, an ion temperature of about 15 keV, and a confinement time of about a second.

The tokamak program

The development of fusion has proven to be extraordinarily difficult. In its early days, many seemingly promising concepts were carefully considered and rejected before settling on the tokamak, now the most highly developed device. A tokamak is a toroidal plasma, which is confined by both, a toroidal magnetic field provided by external coils, a poloidal field produced by the plasma current, and a vertical field used to position the plasma. The plasma has cylindrical symmetry about the vertical axis passing through the center of the horizontal torus.

There have been three large tokamaks, JET in England (set up by the European community) (1), TFTR in Princeton in the United States (2), and JT-60in Japan (3). Large here means that 40 MW of external power, mostly neutral beams, have been used to power them, and that the major radius is at least 2.5 m. Each operates with Mega Amp currents, magnet fields of 3–5.5 T and aspect ratios of about 3 (i.e. about a 3 m major radius and a 1 m minor radius). Maximum electron density in tokamak discharges is typically about 10^{20} m^{-3} and the temperature is around 10 keV. In neutral beam heated discharges, the ion temperature is greater, than the electron temperature. However, in a reactor, which would have larger size, the temperatures are assumed to be about equal.

Two dimensionless parameters characterizing tokamak operation are the β and the q. The former is the plasma pressure divided by the magnetic pressure

$$\beta = 4 \times 10^{-22} n(T_e + T_i)/B^2 \qquad (1)$$

A β related parameter which has proven to be useful is the normalized beta,

$$\beta_n=100\beta aB/I \qquad\qquad (2)$$

Here n is the electron number density in units of m^{-3}, T is the temperature in units of keV, and B is the magnetic field in Teslas, a is the plasma minor radius in meters along the midplane, and I is the current in Mega Amps (MA).

Since the minor radius a is always fixed in a particular tokamak, and the magnetic field B almost always is, the beta is maximized by maximizing the current in a device with a given β_N. However, there are limits on the current also, limiting the beta to typically the range of a few percent up to perhaps 4 percent.

The other dimensionless parameter characterizing tokamak discharges is the q. In the simplest case where the plasma cross section is circular in the poloidal plane, the q is simply defined as

$$q(r)=rB/RB_\theta(r) \qquad\qquad (3)$$

where R is the major radius in meters, r is the minor radius in meters, B is the toroidal field, and B_θ (r) is the poloidal, both in Teslas. Note that as the current increases, so does the poloidal field, and therefore q decreases. Note that q is dependent on minor radius and varies across the plasma cross section. If the cross section is not circular, q^{-1} is the number of loops the poloidal field makes in the poloidal plane when the toroidal field goes around once.

While B, the toroidal field is relatively constant, the density and temperature generally have a strong variation with r, the minor radius. For instance, shown in Figure 4 is an ion temperature, q, and relative pressure plot from JT-60 [3]. Notice that these plots show various regions, the main fusion core, and also what is called the pedestal, a region of the plasma near the separatrix at the edge, and having much lower temperature and density than the main plasma. Notice that in the core plasma, the ion temperature is a rather peaked function of minor radius. The q has a strong variation with r, much of it coming from outside the main heated and current carrying plasma. However Figure 4 shows that at the edge of the hot plasma, the q is about 3.

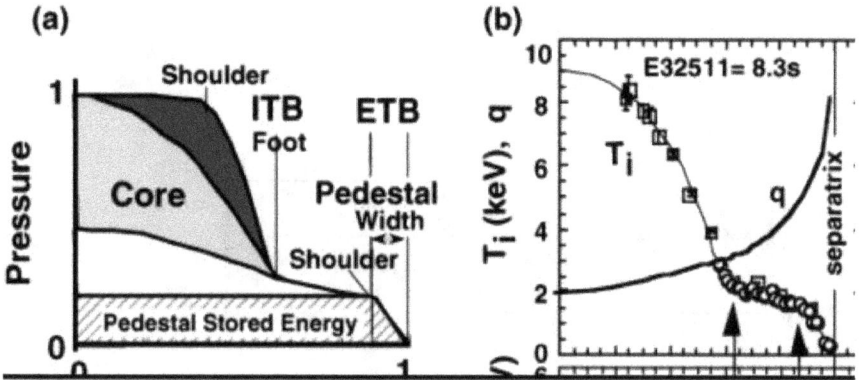

Figure 4. A plot of ion temperature, pressure and q as function of minor radius in a neutral beam heated discharge of JT-60, 8.3 s into the run, taken from Ref (1).

The tokamak is what one calls a two-dimensional configuration, as the plasma has no dependence on the coordinate angle which goes around toroidal axis. A transformer drives the plasma the current. However, the transformer has only so many volt seconds, so at some point the current can no longer be driven. An important area of tokamak research then is finding a steady state (or perhaps pulsed high duty factor) way of driving the current. There has been a great deal of research on driving currents with microwaves, neutral beams, as well as what is called the bootstrap current, a method of current drive inherent in the two-dimensional configuration (a purely cylindrical plasma has no bootstrap current).

Both JT-60, D-3D and other tokamaks have been successful in running quiescent discharges in fusion relevant regimes as long as their power supplies and or volt seconds have held out. Recall that neither of these use superconducting magnets, so the magnetic field requires an enormous amount of power. Figure 5 show plots of β_n for a long (i.e. 30 second) discharge in JT-60 [3,4] and a long (5 s) discharge in D-3D [5].

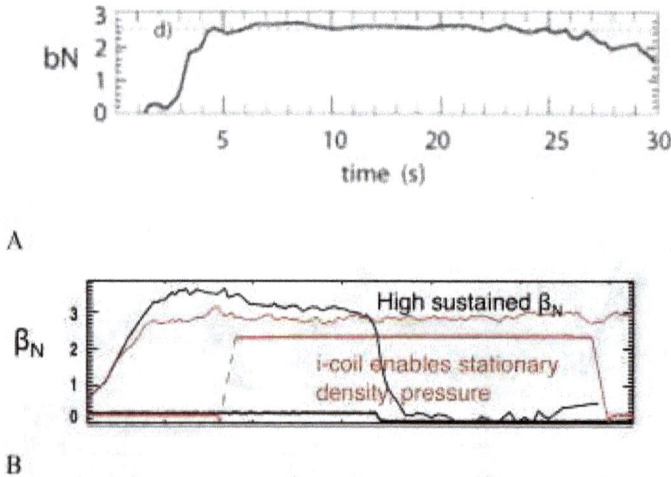

A

B

Figure 5. Plots of the normalized beta in a sustained discharge in A: JT-60 from [3], and B: D-3D, the time axis for D-3D [5] in B goes up to 4.5 s.

Because of the success of tokamaks, the nations doing major MFE research (theUSA, Europe, Russia, China, South Korea, Japan, and India) have joined together to build a much larger Tokamak, ITER. It was originally designed to have a major radius of 8 m, a minor radius of 2.7 m, with the field produced by a superconducting magnet so there will be no power drain from the magnet. It will cost $10B for construction and $1B per year to operate.This ITER, which we now call Large ITER here was designed to achieve Q~10 and generate 1.5 GW of neutron power in a 400 s pulse and have a current of 20 MA [6]. Because of the high cost, the USA pulled out. It rejoined when a smaller, less powerful version (ITER instead of Large ITER) was substituted, one having a major radius of 6 m, a minor radius of 2 m, and had half the cost. It was designed to generate 500 MW of neutron power, still with Q ~ 10 for 400 s and have ~15MA [7]. ITER is now largely constructed in France and is an enormous project; the construction cost was originally estimated at ~$5B, but is now estimated to be at least $25B, possibly higher. It was originally scheduled to be turned on in 2016, but this date has now slipped to at least 2025, with DT experiments to begin about 2035.

Quoting from the ITER web site, its most important goal is to produce 500 MW of fusion power from 50 MW of input power. A schematic of ITER, taken from its web site is shown in Figure (6), taken from the ITER web site (8).

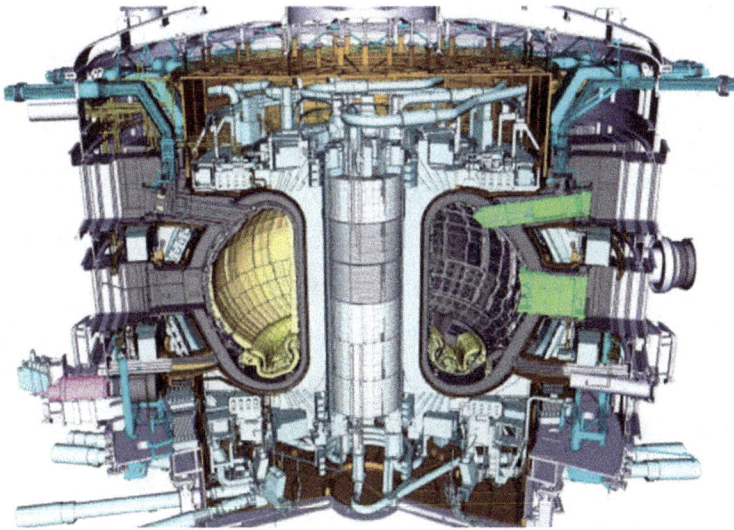

Figure 6. A schematic of ITER taken from its web site. The major radius is 6 meters and the plasma volume will be about 1000 cubic meters. It is expected to use about 50 MW of neutral beam and microwave power to generate about 500 MW of fusion power. (8)

The hope is that ITER will increase the triple product by about an order of magnitude. If successful, it will achieve this mostly by increasing the confinement time to about 10 s, but keeping about the same density and temperature. It is thought that the losses are basically diffusive, or perhaps convective, so they decrease with size of the machine in some way. (For instance, if the losses were radiative and the plasma were optically thin, the losses would be independent of machine size.)

Another problem the tokamak confronts is disruptions; this is the sudden release of the plasma and poloidal magnetic field energy in some uncontrolled manner. A particular potential problem is that a portion of this energy might reside in a decoupled high current, high energy circulating electron beam. This could be generated if the current is driven Ohmically initially, when the density is low. If this beam is present when the plasma disrupts, there is virtually nothing that can stop the energetic electron beam before it hits a wall somewhere, and does great damage. Tokamaks have had a long history of being damaged by disruptions, especially if the damage mechanism is the electron beam, where even one Joule dumped on the wall has, on occasion, done serious damage.

In JET, about 10 MJ of plasma energy (about 5 pounds of TNT) can be released; the poloidal field energy is also released so typically this 10 MJ becomes about 20. A great deal of progress has been made in avoiding disruptions, as we have seen, JT-60 has demonstrated disruption free operation for 30 s, the maximum time of their pulse power, in fusion relevant regimes. However just because the tokamak has run disruption free this long does not mean the problem has been solved, a fusion reactor after all, must run disruption free for months or years.

Note also that ITER has a stored magnetic energy, at the design field of ~5 T, of about 7000 Megajoules, or nearly the energy of about a two-ton bomb. Large ITER would have about twice the stored energy. If the β is about 3 %, assuming it maintains a normalized β of about 2.5 as has been achieved (more later), the plasma energy is about 200 Megajoules. However, the energy available for a disruption also includes the poloidal magnetic field energy, which is roughly equal to the plasma energy. Hence the energy available for a disruption is about 400 MJ, or the energy of a 200-pound bomb, more than the energy in the warhead of the Exocet missile that sank the Sheffield cruiser in the Falkland Island war. It is an enormous energy to release in the confined space of ITER.

But that is only not the only risk. If the disruption, or anything else, should generate an uncontrolled quench of the superconducting magnets, the energy released would be about that of 2 tons of TNT, and this would be enormously destructive. An uncontrolled quench did occur in CERN a few years ago, putting the machine out of commission for over a year. Yet CERN is in a tunnel 10's of km in circumference. An uncontrolled quench in the confined volume of ITER would almost certainly destroy the building and much else. Many measures are taken to prevent uncontrolled quenches, and they occur only very rarely, but they can, and have occurred. My doctor told me that once one of the MRI machines in his hospital quenched, and the whole room quickly filled up with white smoke. This was the quench of about a cubic meter of 3T field. ITER explores an entirely new range of energy. Its 5 T field has a stored energy of about 10 MJ/m^3, so in a 700 m^3 machine that is about 7000 MJ. JT 60, on the other hand, with its 3T field has a stored energy of about 4 MJ/m^3, so in its volume of about 50 m^3, it stores only about 200 MJ.

This is not to say that tokamaks, even of ITER size, are inherently unsafe. The ITER energies mentioned are of about the same order as the kinetic energy of a fully loaded Boeing 747 flying at altitude (~400 metric tons at 300 m/s). However, the air crew can control the plane, and people are inside. The point is to emphasize that the energies involved are great, and before tokamaks can ever become commercial reactors, this energy must be controlled as well as the 747. This will certainly be one of the main tasks for ITER. Can it control the disruptions on a machine this size and obviously, totally avoid uncontrolled quenches?

Hence the two major plasma physics problems which the tokamak confronts, are driving the current steady state, and avoiding disruptions.

L, H and super H modes of tokamak operation

In the earliest days of the tokamak research, the confinement time was regarded as unsatisfactory. There were a variety of phenomenological formulas for the confinement time, as a function of various parameters; the details are unimportant to present here. However, in 1982, the ASDEX tokamak in Germany found that with some increase in beam heating power, the confinement time began to increase, roughly by about a factor of 2 in the best circumstances. Every other tokamak has confirmed this. The original mode was called the L mode, for low confinement; the new mode was called the H mode for high confinement. The numerical multiplicative factor characterizing the improvement over the original formula for confinement time was defined as H, and is typically about a factor of 2. Virtually all planning of future tokamak operation, especially for ITER, assumes H mode operation.

More recently, two American tokamaks, Alcator (as its final experimental campaign before being closed down) and D-3D discovered a new mode called the super H mode [5], which once again roughly doubled the confinement time. The key was increasing the pedestal density and temperature, which they did both by exploiting code predictions, and finding a serpentine path in parameter space which would get them there.

Experiments show that not only does the plasma perform better in the super H mode, but the profiles are also much less peaked. Shown in Figure 7 are temperature and density profiles from both Alcator and D-3D in the super H mode, as well as the magnetic surfaces. The picture is taken from [5], which is published open access.

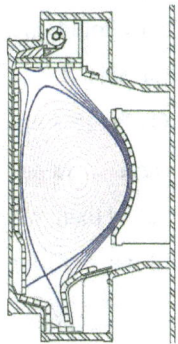

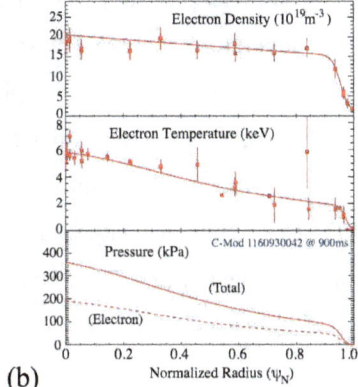

(a)   (b)

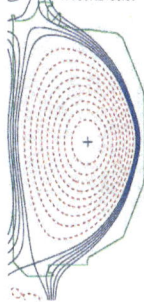

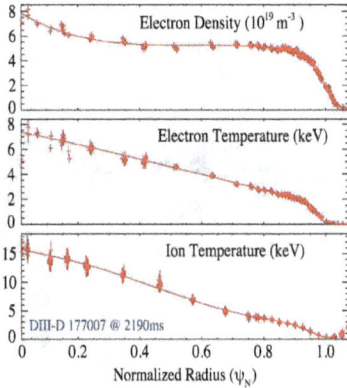

(c)   (d)

Figure 7. a and b: The magnetic surfaces and electron density, temperature, and Pressure in Alcator in the super H mode. c and d, the same for D-3D. Notice that in each case the temperature and density profiles are much broader than what was hitherto typical as in Figure 4. [5]

While these did not run with DT plasmas, they did some of their runs with DD plasmas. From neutron production from these DD plasmas, they could infer what the production probably would have been, had the plasma been DT. This measurement was done on DIII-D, and they came up with a Q of 0.15, impressive for such a small tokamak. Incidentally JT-60, on a much larger tokamak did a similar experiment in 1998. They found that with what they called their W shaped diverter, they achieved an equivalent Q of 1.25. Shown in Figure (8) are these results (9).

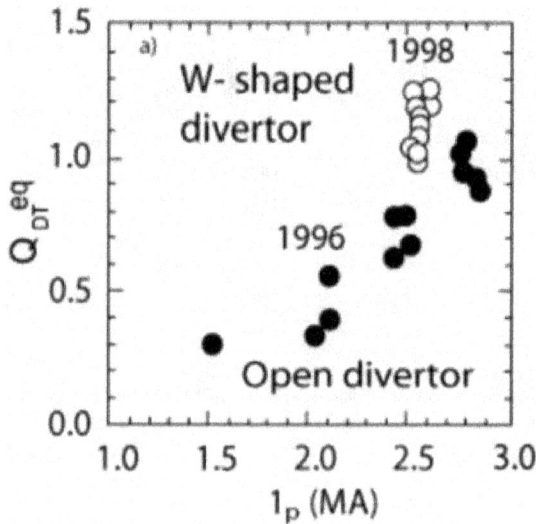

Figure (8) Equivalent DT Q from JT-60 with and without the W shaped divertor [23]. In the latter series of experiments, it achieved a DT equivalent Q of 1.25. (9)

ITER's pure fusion's scientific dilemma

To see ITER's pure fusion's scientific dilemma, let's stipulate the best possible outcome from ITER. Say it achieves Q~10, producing 500 MW of fusion power and had the plasma heated and current driven by 50 MW of beams and/or microwaves soon after 2035. While ITER is an experimental device, not a power plant, let us imagine a power plant having its parameters. Since electricity is typically produced with an efficiency of ~1/3, the device would produce 170 MWe. However, it needs 50 MW to drive it. But beams and microwaves are not produced with 100% efficiency either, again 1/3 is a better estimate, so 150 MWe is needed to drive the tokamak, leaving all of 20MW for the grid! Of course, one could calculate a higher estimate by stipulating higher efficiencies. In fact, higher efficiency power plants have been designed and built. Depending on a new, higher efficiency power plant just to make fusion viable does not sound like a very good argument for either fusion or the new power plant. Up to now, 1/3 is really about right and corresponds to nearly all experience with nuclear power, although as we have seen, some modern coal and most gas powered plants have higher efficiency. Furthermore, the total beam and microwave systems used to heat the plasma and drive its current, struggle to reach even that efficiency. Also regarding ITER, given the size and cost of ITER, even if it were fully ignited and took no external power, its size and cost for 170 MWe would still render the device totally uneconomical.

To make pure fusion economically feasible, first, ITER's Q would have to be increased by at least a factor of 3 or 4, so the circulating power is a much smaller fraction of the total. Secondly, the device would have to be made smaller and cheaper while increasing the power by at least a factor of 5 or 6 (a typical power plant has about 3 GW thermal (GWth) and about 1 GW electric (GWe) power). As we will see in the next sub section, this means operating in regions of parameter space that tokamaks have not typically been able to operate in. Finally, since the device would be both smaller and more powerful, the neutron wall loading, and the plasma divertor loading, would be at least an order of magnitude greater. These are not minor details; almost certainly, they would take decades and decades, and tens and tens of billions of dollars to achieve, assuming they could be achieved at all. The ITER web site dismisses all of this by saying that after ITER, there will be the next fusion device, the DEMO which will provide commercial power. Who knows what this is, how much it will cost, or how long it will take. At best pure fusion could be a 22nd century power source if developed along the ITER development route. But the need could well be for sustainable power much sooner. As we will see shortly, a fusion reactor having Large ITER, or even ITER like parameters could be fine for an economical fusion breeder, if not for an economical pure fusion reactor.

Conservative design rules

As described in Refs. (10-14) and in their references, and elaborated in Ref (15), tokamaks are constrained in the current, pressure and density they can contain. Freidberg has derived similar constraints (14). We have called these conservative design rules (CDR's). Conservative design rules are well-known constraints on tokamaks operation; they are not controversial, they have been known for years, and have been well confirmed experimentally. They are discussed in detail in (10-12). However, the tokamak community has been loath to put them all together and see that they provide serious constraints on what a tokamak reactor can and cannot do.

These CDR's are expressed as limits on tokamak parameters:

βN < 2.5 (the normalized beta) (4)

If this condition is violated, the plasma will be unstable to what are called ballooning modes (16,17).

$q_{95} > 3$ (the q at the magnetic surface containing 95% of the plasma current. It is proportional to the reciprocal of the plasma current). It is also called the safety factor. If this condition is violated, the plasma will be unstable to what are called tearing modes (18-20).

$n < 0.75 \, n_G$ (the Greenwald density). The Greenwald density is an empirical density limit which all tokamak plasmas seem to obey (21, 22)

The blanket must be at least a meter thick, preferably a meter and a half, to contain all the 14 MeV neutrons and prevent leakage out the back.

The name conservative is used because if the first 3 are violated, the result is generally a major disruption. If the last is violated, it is not clear that the wall can contain enough 14 MeV neutrons, and an unacceptable number may well leak out the back. Generally, this means the tokamak must operate in a region of parameter space defined by these 'conservative design rules'. This was first pointed out by the author in 2009 (10), and extended by Freidberg et al. (14)

Since a major disruption is obviously something to be avoided in a tokamak reactor, its design must be conservative as regards these parameters. These limits are not controversial; they have a solid base in theory and have been confirmed in a wide variety of experiments. Every large tokamak has been constrained by them. For instance, the nature of a large number of discharges in JT-60 have been plotted out in the $q_{95}b_N$ plane shown in Fig. (9). (3)

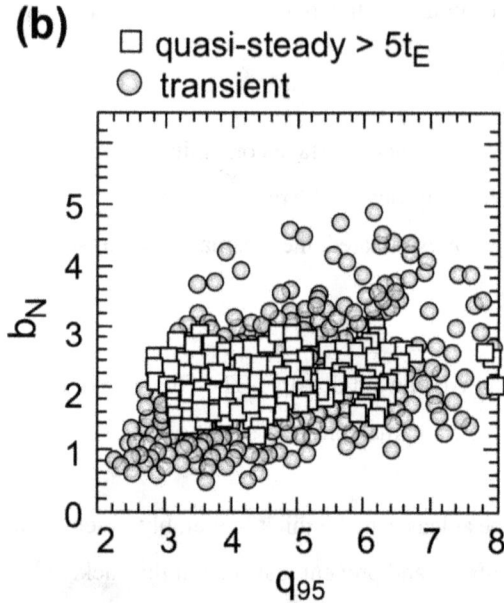

(b)

□ quasi-steady > $5t_E$
○ transient

Figure (9) : A plot in (b_N q_{95} space) of aspects of a large number of discharges in JT-60. The blank squares represent discharges that have lasted at least 5 energy confinement times, the shaded circles are discharged that did not, i.e. discharges marked as transient. Clearly steady state is only achievable for q_{95} > 3 and b_N < 2.5, just as predicted by conservative design rules. (3)

Notice that JT-60 has also gotten discharges with high b_N, as high as 5 for q_{95} of 6 and for q_{95} as low as 2, for b_N about 1. However, these constitute no improvement in the actual beta, which is proportional to b_N times the current, or to b_N/ q_{95}. In addition, these all disrupt in less than 5 energy confinement times.

The European tokamak JET also showed very similar results. They measured a quantity the called the disruptivity, the reciprocal of average time between major disruptions as a function of both q^{-1} and density. Their graphs, taken from (23) are shown in Figure (10).

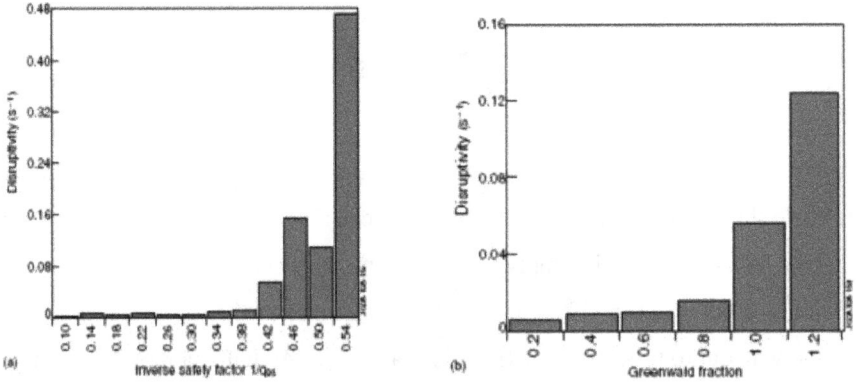

Figure (10) Plot of the disruptivity as a function of q^{-1} and fraction of Greenwald density taken from JET (23).

Notice that all these graphs, from 2 of the 3 largest tokamaks basically confirm conservative design rules. However even if q ~3, the disruptivity is ~ 10^{-2}, namely a disruption every two minutes, obviously not satisfactory for a reactor. Hopefully when ITER is constructed, there will be more and better information available. If ITER can routinely run disruption free for 7 minutes (400 sec), it will be a major accomplishment.

The CDR's put a serious limit on the fusion power. This was calculated in two ways for two different assumptions on profiles. The first calculation was motivated by beam heated tokamaks, where the ion temperature is about twice the electron temperature. Since these tokamaks are all assumed to be pressure limited, the fusion power maximizes at the assumed ion temperature of ~ 17keV. Parabolic spatial profiles in the poloidal plane were assumed for all densities and temperatures. This gave the power limit in (10). However, a more realistic approach is to assume equal temperatures, in other words, it is necessary to replace some of the ion pressure which reacts, with electron pressure with does not. This reduces the expression in (10) by a factor of 9/16, giving a limit for the fusion power of

127

$$P < 0.06 \ \kappa^2 \ [aB]^4/R \qquad\qquad (5)$$

Alternatively, one assumes much more uniform profiles as measured in the super H mode shots. Furthermore, for the beta, one can make the optimistic assumption that the beta in all cases is simply the maximum value achieved in any case, ~4%. That gives the result in (12). However, that assumes profiles constant in radius all the way out to the separatrix (i.e. plasma edge). Actually, a more reasonable approximation, as suggested by Fig (7) is a uniform profile out to about 80% of the plasma edge, and then a rapid drop off. This would reduce the fusion power by ~64%, leading to

$$P < 2x10^{-3} \ p^2 \ \kappa \ Ra^2 \ B^4 \qquad\qquad (6)$$

Equation (5) is a more pessimistic estimate, Eq. (6) more optimistic.

Now let us consider a 3GW tokamak (like a conventional power plant), taking κ=1.7 (the ellipticity in the poloidal plane), and a = R/3. Then Eqs. (1-2) become formulas for the minimum radius R, as a function of the magnetic field. These are summarized in Table (2). The left-hand column specifies the magnetic field, 5 or 9 T, the top row, R, from Eqs. (1-2). The Table entries are the minimum radii in meters (rounded to the nearest whole number).

B	R [Eq(2)]	R [Eq(1)]
5	11	12
9	5	6

TABLE 2: Minimum major radius in meters for a 3 GW fusion power tokamak as calculated by CDR's for fields of 5 and 9T.

Consider a 5T power plant. The entire device, counting the field coils and shielding would extend from the goal line to about the 30–35-yard line of an American football field. It simply does not seem that this would be affordable for every power station.

Now let us see what this means for neutron power production. We consider TFTR and JET, which have actually produced fusion power, and ITER, ARC, and Large ITER, which are on the drawing boards and which may well be built. Assuming that the maximum stable current is given, as it nearly always is for the particular tokamak, and that it is low enough that the profile is tearing mode stable, we can get the average beta by assuming a maximum β_N of 2.5. For all the devices we have been considering, the maximum beta calculated this way is less than 4%. Hence we use Eq. (5) for the CDR limited power; the results are in Table 3. Details of the DT experiments in both JET and TFTR are summarized in Ref.s (1,2 and 12).

Tokamak	B	I	a	b	$P_{cdr}(\beta = 0.04)$	$P_{a\ or\ d}$
TFTR[a](2)	5.6	2.7	0.9	0.013	63	10
JET[b](1)	3.5	4.8	1.25	0.03	12	8
ITER (7)	5	15	2	0.038	800	500
ARC (39)	9	8	1.1	0.02	1400	700
Large ITER (6)	5.7	20	2.8	0.031	3600	1500

a.For TFTR the power is given for the hot ion mode

b. For JET the power is given for the thermal mode.

Table 3. The columns specifies the particular tokamak, The magnetic field in Teslas, the current in MA, the minor radius along the horizontal plane in meters, the β, assuming $\beta_N = 2.5$, the neutron power as predicted by conservative design rules (Eq. 5), and the actual power (TFTR and JET) or design power (the others). ARC is a high field tokamak proposed by MIT and Commonwealth Fusion to be discussed shortly

It is likely that in the hot ion mode, TFTR has a very nonthermal ion distribution, and many of the neutrons are produced by beam plasma reactions. In a large thermal reactor, even if heated with neutral beams, this is unlikely to occur, as the beam slowing down rate greatly exceeds the beam ion fusion rate In any case, in TFTR, the hot ion mode does not seem to be able to access the high power possible in a thermal plasma. Notice the TFTR, with its higher magnetic field than JET, and the B^4 scaling of power would seemingly be able to achieve considerably higher power. Unfortunately, the machine was taken down before this advantage could be further investigated and possibly exploited.

While the hot ion mode is almost certainly not a thermal, Maxwellian plasma, it could be possible to exploit non thermal plasmas in other ways. If the fusion alpha particles can be convinced to heat the ions, rather than electrons, this would increase the fusion rate. This has been explored by Fisch et al [24] and is called alpha channeling. Some rf is injected into the plasma in such a way as to transfer energy from the alphas to the ions. If the ions can be maintained at twice the electron temperature, i.e. $T_i = 16keV$ and $T_e = 8keV$, then at the pressure limit, the electron density would be increased by a factor of 4/3, and the fusion power by 16/9.

However, the conservative design rules give rise to a real limit on neutron power, which TFTR and JET seem to be constrained by. For the JET thermal plasma, the conservative design rules predict more than the actual neutron power, and both the design powers of ITER and ARC are well under what conservative design rules would allow.

Over the past 20 years, this author has suggested (to no avail) that the American magnetic fusion program, concentrate its resources on building a tokamak he has called the 'scientific prototype' [24-29]. This is a tokamak about the size of JT-60U, but would run at steady state or high duty cycle, with a DT plasma, and have a Q~1. As we have seen, this has already been achieved in a 30 second pulse in JT-60U with its W shaped divertor in a deuterium plasma. The scientific prototype, in DT, would also produce its own tritium. Furthermore, since only a small fraction of the tritium in the tokamak burns before it escapes, it would have to recover this tritium for reuse. If in a first experiment of this type, it could not produce enough tritium to fuel itself, it would produce as much as it could; same for tritium recovery. In short, no matter how successful ITER is, there are problems which it must solve, which it has hardly beginning to address.

The idea of the scientific prototype is to address (and hopefully solve) these problems on as small a scale as possible. The scientific prototype will be expensive, but not beyond the means of countries like the United States, China, Japan or the European Union. If we do not address these problems now, when will we? The hope would be to achieve the goals of the scientific prototype around 2040, just as ITER hopefully is successful in achieving a Q~10 machine. The fact that we know what has been done in JT-60U would certainly simplify the design process. We would like to use a tokamak that produces essentially the same plasma, but in DT instead of just deuterium. Of course, a large part of the design would be hardening the reactor to deal with the tritium and 14 MeV neutrons, as well as producing tritium and recovering unburned tritium.

Had the American fusion program built the scientific prototype 20 years ago as proposed then [25,26], the world would probably now have a reasonably good idea of its success or failure. Instead, the American magnetic fusion program spun its wheels proposing one ignition scheme or new plasma configuration, after another, none of which got built or funded.

While the author's efforts to advocate the scientific prototype have been focused on the United States, there is no reason it cannot be set up in any of the main sponsors of ITER. This author does not advocate that the scientific prototype be done by an international consortium. The international negotiations to pull this off, would probably take up most of the time between now and 2040.

If both the scientific prototype and ITER are successful by ~2040, there is no reason why fusion breeding cannot be begun on a large scale. On the other hand, if the world's choice is to continue with pure fusion, it would be on the next plateau in that effort.

One assumption in the argument for the scientific prototype was that the plasma current could be driven externally by microwaves, millimeter waves and/or neutral beams. Recent results from a variety of tokamaks have called this assumption into question.

The need for a steady state tokamak has hardly escaped the world's attention. In 1993, the PPPL put in a proposal for a steady state tokamak called tokamak physics experiment, or TPX [30]. This was proposed to be a tokamak which had its current driven only externally, by beams and/or microwaves, as well as by a characteristic of the toroidal geometry called bootstrap current.

TPX was designed with a 2.25-meter major radius and R/a=4.5. It was to have a superconducting magnet with a toroidal field of 4 Teslas, and have a plasma current of 2 MA. It was designed for initially 20 MW of heating and current drive power, and ultimately 50 MW It desired to show efficient current drive without an Ohmic current, one disruption every 10 hours of operation, initially 100 second pulses, ultimately 1000 second. It hoped to achieve an average density of $\sim 10^{20}$m^{-3}, a temperature of 10-20 keV, a confinement time of $\sim$350msec, and a triple product of $3-5 \times 10^{20}$.   The triple product expected was to be a factor of 3 to 5 below the record set on JT-60, but with long pulse and external current drive, it would make many records in other ways.

Unfortunately, TPX was never built. The proposal was ultimately abandoned in favor of a variety of proposals for burning plasmas, which were also never built. Instead, the Princeton lab settled for paper studies for stellarators, even though it is currently a secondary fusion configuration and the Germans and Japanese programs were far ahead. It also and built a spherical tokamak, which this author argued will never provide economical fusion due to a thin center post, which almost certainly cannot stand up long to the fusion neutron flux, much less remain superconducting [27].

However other laboratories have built superconducting tokamaks in the interim, Tore Supra in France [31], KSTAR (Korea superconducting tokamak advanced reactor) in Korea [32], and EAST (experimental advanced superconducting tokamak) in China [33, 34]. These have been up and running for quite a while and have been powered by $\sim$10 MW of microwaves and beams. There have been stories in the major media, especially regarding the latter two, of maintaining high temperatures (i.e. $\sim$10keV) for a hundred or more seconds, maintained only by

133

external beam and microwave power [35]. Figure 11 shows the loop voltage on a 60 second run from EAST [32].

shot 67341/USN W divertor

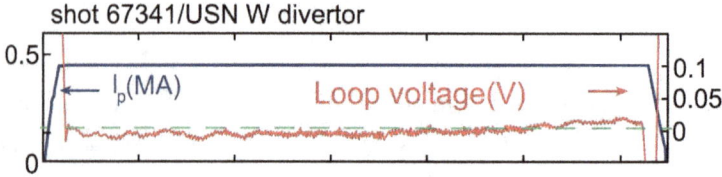

Figure 11 : A plot of toroidal current and loop voltage in a 60 discharge from EAST. Notice that the loop voltage is zero for virtually the entire time. (32)

However, while these tokamaks have certainly achieved impressive results, they have come nowhere near matching the hoped-for results of TPX.

Here we very briefly review some of these results. Perhaps first and foremost, the best triple product up to now turned out to be 10^{19} [34], at least a factor of 150 less than what was achieved on JT-60U and about a factor of 30-50 less than what TPX hoped to achieve. In fact Ohmically driven tokamaks had achieved this triple product more than 40 years ago. One reason is that the density and temperatures are lower than what TPX hoped to achieve (and what JT-60U did achieve). Not only that, as seen in Fig 12, [34], the density and temperature are rather peaked, and using the central density and temperature, rather than the radial average, gives a rather optimistic estimate of triple product. In fact, the stored plasma energy in both EAST and KSTAR varies from about 100 to 400kJ [32-34]. This is considerably less than the nearly 10 MJ stored in JT-60.

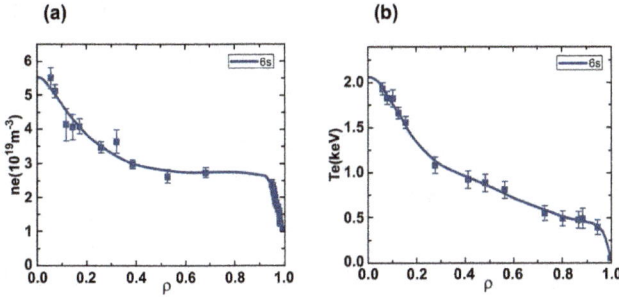

(a) **(b)**

Figure 12 : Radial plots of electron density and temperature in a typical shot of the EAST tokamak . The stored energy in EAST and KSTAR vary with shot between about 100kJ and 400kJ. (33)

The rather lower energy in EAST and KSTAR, along with the 5-10 MW of input power mean that the energy confinement time is quite small, perhaps 50 milliseconds. The combination of low stored energy and low confinement time result in a triple fusion project much smaller than what had been achieved on many other tokamaks.

Tore Supre published some data on the statistics of disruptions. Their measure is the disruption frequency, which was always well above a rate of one every 10 hours. Shown in Figure 13 is their plot [31].

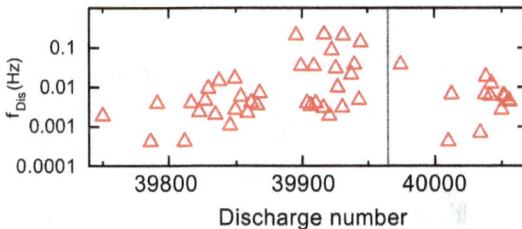

Figure 13 : A scatter plot of the frequency of disruptions for a large number of shots. Note that a disruption rate of one every 10 hours would be a frequency of ~3×10^{-5}. (31)

135

The best disruption frequency Tore Supra had achieved is an order of magnitude higher than what TPX aimed for.

In this author's opinion, the results from these 3 superconducting tokamaks have been rather discouraging, at least as regards the potential of external current drive. But where does this leave the scientific prototype? Some insight can be derived from [36]. This work examines the comparison of a pulsed tokamak, with mostly Ohmic current drive, with a steady state tokamak with external current drive. This work is focused on a future tokamak which is providing economic power. Each half cycle is expected to be an hour to an hour and a half. However, the goals of the scientific prototype are much more modest.

One thing which Ref. [36] does not discuss is the current waveform, that is the magnetic flux as a function of time over several cycles. However, judging from the paper, the switch from clockwise to counterclockwise toroidal current seems to be assumed instantaneous. This is a switch from one MHD equilibrium to another, with an intermediate state having no MHD equilibrium (i.e. zero toroidal current means no MHD equilibrium) in between. Once the current is zero, the remaining unconfined plasma will splash out into the vacuum wall nearly instantaneously. Surely there must be some time for the current to make the switch, as well as to clean out the remaining residue of the unconfined plasma.

This work sees the main goal of the scientific prototype as achieving steady state or high duty cycle power, an making an initial stab at breeding tritium and recovering unburned tritium. It does not have to achieve 100% on the first try. Accordingly, it would modify that assumed in [36], by assuming an initial temporal current profile which rises, and then stays constant for a long time, providing equilibrium for the plasma, and then reverses. Let us consider current on time, t(shot), of 100 seconds and a t(relax) of 500 seconds, where the remnants of the unconfined plasma are swept away, and the system is prepared for the next equilibrium having a reversed current. In other words, the initial scientific prototype would aim for a duty cycle of ~17%. The tokamak plasma would be one very much like JT-60U which has already demonstrated Q=1.25 in a 30 second shot.

The current would be driven mostly by the central transformer, but the project could certainly continue research on external current drive so that if there is further success, one could switch to it. Furthermore, it could work on extending t(shot) and reducing t(relax). If it could reverse the two from what is assumed above (i.e. achieve a duty cycle of ~83%) , it would be just about as good as true steady state. A schematic of the time development of the central flux is shown in Figure 14 for both the reactor and the scientific prototype.

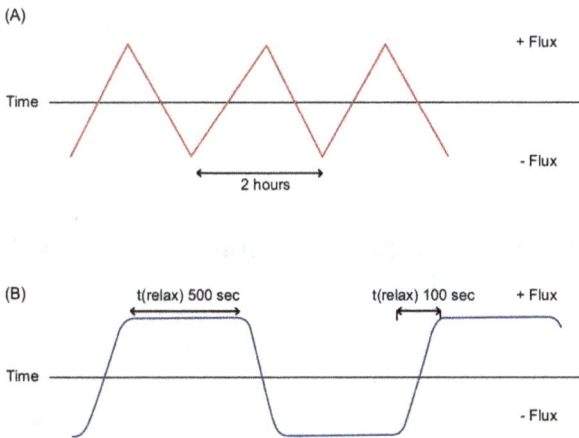

Figure 14: The temporal profile of the tokamak's central flux for A: The pulsed reactor proposed in Ref [36] in red, and B: The first realization of the scientific prototype in blue.

Regarding the plasma, this section emphasized the similarity with that obtained in JT-60. This similarity certainly gives confidence that the scientific prototype can be achieved, at least regarding the plasma. However, the tokamak itself would be very different from JT-60. First of all, it would need room for a blanket, adding at least a meter to the major radius, and likely increasing the minor radius as well. Secondly, in order to breed tritium on site, it would need a flowing blanket, most likely a molten salt like FLiBe, where the flow is in and out of the vacuum system, so the tritium could be removed as it is produced. At a later stage, it might be worth adding some thorium to the flow to produce some ^{233}U. For the first time, the fusion project would be producing something the world could actually use. Finally, it would have to capture as much unburned tritium as possible. Zakharov [37] has proposed doing this by flowing liquid lithium along the divertor plates (outside the region of confined plasma) and ultimately out of the vacuum system. These would absorb some or all of the tritium escaping the plasma.

To summarize, the scientific prototype would provide crucial data on running a tokamak at high duty cycle before ITER even begins to be concerned with such matters. If all goes well, it might even be able to this work at steady state, or at much higher duty cycle. It would provide crucial data necessary for fusion, which could not be achieved in any other way.

Fusion start-ups' pilot plants all have serious problems and will most likely fail

In the last few years, many private companies, generally called 'fusion start ups', have sprung up. They claim, nearly universally, that they will have fusion on the grid much quicker than the national labs, generally within about a bit more than a decade. They have achieved wide recognition, and in March 2022 there was even a White House conference on their approach to fusion. At the conference, the fact that rapid development of fusion would solve the climate crisis played center stage. Here is a portion of Gina McCarthy's talk while hosting the conference (38):

Gina McCarthy, White House National Climate Advisor, spoke about the ways the Biden-Harris Administration is addressing climate change, such as a commitment to get to 100% carbon-free electricity by …..

Needless to say, the various 'fusion start ups' snapped at the bait. Here are two quotes typical of very many:

General Fusion web site: With the urgency of climate change in mind, we are on course to power homes, businesses, and industry with fusion energy by the 2030s.

TAE press release: "We're here today because the world is on fire. Because generations before us made bold investments to give us the first solutions to this crisis. Because we must act. And we believe that when it comes to fusion, the time is now."

This manuscript asserts that thinking of fusion hooked up to the grid in ~10 years is a pipe dream. The effort is simply not ready for prime time, there is too much unknown to get from where we are now, to electricity for the grid in the time these companies promise. In fact, given the lack of a 'climate crisis', they are peddling a non-solution to a non-problem, this nearly immediate non-solution, which will fail, will cost billions (but to private investors, who probably should know better).

This author is certainly not opposed to private companies ultimately getting involved in fusion once the time is right. In fact, ultimately, they will be essential, but the time is not now. Consider the situation in space capable rockets, where private companies in the United States are now eclipsing NASA rockets (in fact originally Army and Navy rockets). But NASA rockets were the only game in town for about 50 years, and NASA made enormous gains in developing these rockets with little input from the private sector for about half a century. Only then, when much of the technology was largely established by NASA, could the prospect of further development be more certain, and in a shorter time, so that investors could reap profits within a reasonable time horizon if the project were to be successful. Only then could private companies come in and begin to take over. Fusion is nowhere near where space rockets were even as early as in 1957 when satellites began to circle the earth. After all, rocket work began decades before 1957. We have not even launched our fusion analog of Sputnik yet. Private companies could not take over space rockets in 1956; private companies cannot take over fusion now.

These fusion companies are supported by private dollars, and the dollars invested are large. Helion brags that it has attracted $2.2B; Commonwealth Fusion, $1.8B; TAE, ~ $1B. These companies, of course, can spend their private $$$ any way they wish, but if their investors expect a payoff in the next decade, they are in for a big disappointment.

While with their large dollar amount, they will undoubtedly make some contributions to fusion science and technology, this author thinks their overall impacts will be harmful. They are raising unrealistic expectations, which will further degrade fusion's already weak credibility. Who knows what the effect will be when these efforts all collapse with a gigantic splat. Will they take down the normal, government sponsored fusion effort with them, thereby destroying a potentially very important project? Quite possibly.

Why will these efforts most likely fail?

Commonwealth Fusion: This company, a spin off from the MIT program, is probably the only one that could have succeeded in going the normal government sponsored route. They have published their designs in the open literature (39), so it is entirely appropriate for readers to offer scientific analysis of their design, and if appropriate criticism, also in the open scientific literature. They have a new technology that could allow tokamaks to operate at larger magnetic fields, 9-10T instead of 3-5T. The Princeton Plasma Physics Lab (PPPL) at one point was interested in purchasing these field coils to do their own experiments with them. Commonwealth has plans for a small tokamak called SPARC, which they hope demonstrates high gain, and a larger one called ARC which they will hope will deliver commercial power in a decade or so. The company has been rather open and has published a considerable amount of its work.

Regarding the plasma, the higher magnetic fields are an unquestioned benefit, but, they are a double edge sword. An economical fusion source is more than just the plasma, and for these other components, the high field is a drawback. As the size shrinks and the power increases, the wall loading increases. SPARC and ARC would have higher wall loading than ITER, and wall loading is a serious problem area for ITER. Not only that, unlike ARC, ITER is a pulsed machine, and does not have to operate steady state to supply power to the grid. Table 4 gives the radius in meters, field in T, the power and the neutron wall loading for ITER, SPARC, and ARC, taken from the ITER web site, as well as the Commonwealth papers just cited.

Machine	R (M)	B(T)	P(MW)	loading (MW/m^2)
ITER	6	5	500	0.7 (pulsed)
SPARC	1.65	>10	50	0.8 (steady state)
ARC	3.3	9	500	2.3 (steady state)

TABLE 4, The major radius, magnetic field, fusion power, and neutron wall loading, as expected for several tokamaks.

Notice that SPARC will have more wall loading than ITER, and ARC, considerably more. So far, no tokamak, or any other fusion reactor, has operated with any neutron wall loading at all. To think that ARC and SPARC can operate steady state with higher wall loading than a pulsed ITER, is optimistic, to say the least.

Perhaps even more important, neither ITER, nor SPARC, nor ARC knows at this point how it will drive current steady state. ITER, and most tokamaks drive the current with a transformer, the plasma being the secondary. But the transformer can only drive so many Volt seconds and then the current stops. ITER's pulse time will be 400 seconds and it does not seem to have plans for steady state operation. Of course, ARC and SPARC expect to do just this. Commonwealth's plans are to drive a steady state current externally with microwaves and rf. However, as we have seen, a great deal of experimental data is now in, and it is not encouraging. The Korean tokamak KSTAR and the Chinese, EAST have both driven current for long periods of time externally. The problem is that it takes a great deal more power to drive the current than would be acceptable for economic fusion.

While the final results on external current drive are not necessarily in, and future results may be more encouraging, MIT is currently backing away from external current drive, and is considering having the current oscillate back and forth in direction with a period of perhaps on the order of an hour in each toroidal direction (36). However, when the current goes through zero, there is no MHD equilibrium, and the plasma will splash onto the walls, virtually instantaneously on the time scale of the current waveform. Who knows how long it will take to clean up the mess? In other words, Commonwealth claims its tokamak will provide power to the grid in in a decade, but there are serious uncertainties about how it will drive the current.

Then there is the issue of heating and (maybe) current drive. It will be driven by ICRH (ion cyclotron resonance heating) in SPARC. Inside the plasma, shown in pink in Fig. (15) in their schematic of SPARC, is the belt used to drive the rf power (39). However, there is no physical structure between the plasma and the belt which can protect it from the intense flux of 14 MeV fusion neutrons, which as we have just seen will be nearly a megawatt per m^2 if the experiment is successful. Can the belt stand up to such punishment without losing its electrical properties, and perhaps even its mechanical properties? To this author, it seems far-fetched. However, it is not up me to prove that it cannot survive in that environment, it is up to the designers of SPARC to prove that it can. The only way for them to do so is to show such a current carrying wire or belt that has stood up to such a neutron flux for relevant times.

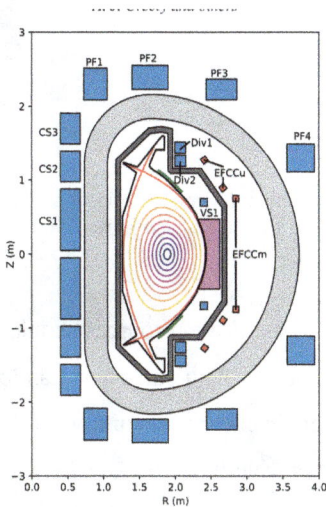

Figure (15): A schematic of the poloidal cross section of SPARC taken from Ref. (50). The pink part inside the vacuum chamber is the belt which carries the current rf current used for ion cyclotron heating. (39)

Seeing the belt inside the vacuum chamber, which must carry a large oscillating current exposed to the neutron flux reminds one of a series of very rough hand drawn cartoons Professor David Rose of MIT circulated in the late 1960's and early 1970's, when I was a graduate student and junior faculty member at MIT. I do not remember all of them, but the one on rf heating was particularly revealing and humorous in this context. Figure (16) is the author's hand drawn recollection of it.

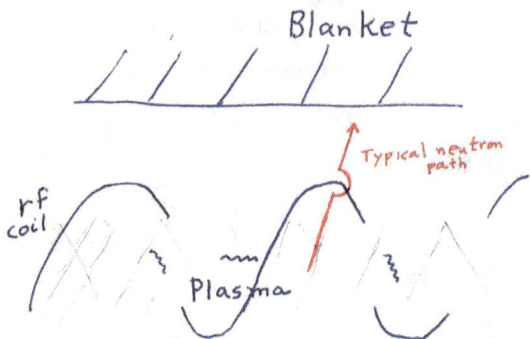

Figure (16): RF heater's view of fusion. Redrawn from memory from a collection of hand drawn cartoons and captions that Professor David Rose of MIT circulated in the 1960's and 1970's.

To this author's mind, the plasma heating (and current drive?) sources should be neutral beams and ECRH. These are the only sources with sufficient standoff. All other sources have key vulnerable components inside the vacuum vessel and are exposed to intense neutron fluxes. Who knows what the effect of a long term $1MW/m^2$ flux of 14 MeV neutrons on these antennas, waveguides, coils or belts will be.

Note also that the thickness of the vacuum wall in SPARC is about half a meter, and this is for a steady state fusion reactor. Conservative design rules specify a meter and a half. ITER with lesser wall loading on a pulsed reactor has a thicker vacuum wall. In short, no matter how small you can make the tokamak plasma, the necessity for a wall of ~1.5 meters thick gives a minimum for how small it is reasonable to make the plasma. Neutron leakage out the back may well be a problem for SPARC.

Speaking of heating, if SPARC achieves a Q~10, then 20% of the fusion power will be from 3.5 MeV doubly charged alpha particles which tend to stay in the machine. There has been no experimental work on significant alpha heating in any magnetic confinement device, although undoubtedly there have been paper studies. What is required? Does anyone know? Do all the alphas have to be removed? Some of them? Can their heating be controlled in any way? How would one do this? Surely there should be some experimental work on this issue before barging ahead with an industrial facility reliant on it.

Finally, the design of ARC makes some rather optimistic assumptions of the various efficiecies. It assume an efficiency of 40% for conversion of fusion power to electrical power. While this is reasonable for the most modern coal fired ultra super critical plants, and modern gas fired plants do even better, existing nuclear power plants typically are stuck around a more standard efficiency of ~1/3. Furthermore their rf and microwave sources are assumed to have an efficiency of 42% conversion from source to power injected into the plasma. This is also a rather optimistic assumption. Making a more conservative assumption, and taking the 2 efficiencies of 33% and 25%, their power to the grid drops from ~300MW to ~ 100MW. The design of ARC is walking delicately on the edge of a cliff in parameter space; drop the efficiency numbers a little, and the power to the grid drops a lot.

To summarize, ARC needs 5 miracles in the next 10 years. These are: running steady state with higher wall loading than any other fusion devices including ITER, figuring our how to drive the current, figuring out how to control the alpha heating, operating with vital unshielded components exposed to the intense neutron flux inside the vacuum vessel, and walking right along the edge of a steep cliff in parameter space where a false step could be catastrophic.

Yet as best this author can discern, due to the potential benefit of higher toroidal field, Commonwealth Fusion's plans make make more sense than those of many of the other 'start ups'.

The General Atomic group has also proposed an advanced tokamak based pilot plant, (40) and this author has published an article skeptical of their chances of success, and even suggested that they try breeding instead; it is much easier (41). The GA response has also been published (42).

Another open controversy in the scientific literature involves TAE (formerly Tri alpha energy). At the earliest stages of TAE, this author was involved. Before getting private $$$ to form their company, Rostoker, Binderbauer and Monkhorst attempted to sell it to ONR (office of naval research) as a means of ship propulsion (43). In their first publication on the subject, they even showed a schematic of a sailor in front of the reactor. Their scheme was a reversed field pinch and their reaction was the p-^{11}B reaction. This reaction has much lower cross section than DT, and required much more energetic fuel particles. It produces 3 alpha particles, the reason for the company's original name. They planned to use beams at the energy that maximized the reaction cross section.

ONR turned their proposal to NRL to review, and NRL gave the job to Martin Lampe and me. We spent months studying their proposal, and our conclusion was that their scheme made absolutely no sense. The number of miracles it needed was almost too large to count. We documented our analysis in an NRL Memorandum report (44) but decided not to publish it in the archival literature. The NRL memo is available either from NRL or from the author. ONR decided not to fund the project. It is now 25 years since their article was published, and still no commercial fusion reactor.

Other 'start ups' include many additional plasma confinement schemes. For instance there is a concept of a spherical tokamak. To this author's mind, this has all the problems of the other tokamaks mentioned here, plus a few more. The idea is to shrink a tokamak down to basically a spherical shape. Topologically it is still a torus, but with an aspect ratio of about unity. It has an advantages in that it can run at higher beta. This means that there will be a thin superconducting center conductor, but carrying the current of all the toroidal coils, and which will be bombarded by the full flux of the fusion neutrons.

Several, including TAE think in terms of a field reversed configuration (FRC). It would be wonderful if this could work, it is an ideal geometrical configuration, but so far their triple fusion product is several orders of magnitude below what JT-60 has achieved. One 'start up' even thinks in terms of this configuration, but with a D-^{3}He plasma, fueled by a D-D reaction. But the D-^{3}He reaction has about 10% of the reaction rate as D-T and the D-D another factor of 10 below the .D-^{3}He reaction. See Figure 2.

Other's think of an FRC, but compressed by an imploding metal liner. This configuration had been analyzed by NRL, and especially Los Alamos over the last 50 years, but has never been built by either lab. Another assures us that we can have heavy ion beam inertial fusion quickly. However, this has been analyzed for over 30 years by the Lawrence Berkeley National lab, but neither the ion accelerator nor the necessary storage rings (enormous components) have ever been built.

In short, the few 'start up' configurations that have been publicly analyzed, are extremely controversial, to say the least. Not one has yet produced even a single

14 MeV neutron, a minimum of 10^{21} per second are needed for an economical fusion device. Others have not been analyzed publicly, but seem to need tremendous advances from where we are now.

Inertial Fusion

Almost as soon after lasers were invented, scientists thought of them as drivers for inertial fusion. Initially the thought was to simply deposit the energy in a target, heat it to fusion temperature and let it fuse. However, the laser energy needed was enormous, many, many megajoules. A significant theoretical breakthrough came when Nuckolls showed that by ablatively compressing the target, the laser energy could be greatly reduced, perhaps to as low as 10 kJ or less [45]. Ablative compression means is that the laser deposits its energy in the outer region of the target, which heats up, ablates away, and the inverse rocket force compresses the remainder of the target to fusion conditions.

The details of the compression are quite complex. For our purposes here, we consider an initial phase where the inner target accelerates inward due to the greatly increasing pressure of the outer part of the target. Once a maximum inward velocity is reached, the laser is turned off and the target coasts inward until it reaches maximum compression at what is called the 'bang time'. At this point, fusion begins very locally in a small spot in the center. The fusion neutrons escape, but the alpha particles are absorbed locally and heat the surrounding parts of the target. The idea is that this sets up a burn wave, analogous to a chemical fire burn wave, and the remainder of the target begins to fuse as it is heated by the burn wave. Notice that once the burn wave starts, the laser is no longer required. The laser only plays the role of 'the magic match'. Also notice that alpha heating is not an afterthought in laser fusion, as it is in tokamak fusion; it is built into the laser fusion culture at the ground floor. That is; no alpha heating, no laser fusion. Magnetic fusion would probably be happier if there were no energetic alphas produced; they only give ~20% of the fusion power, and they complicate thing quite a bit; they not sure what the heck to do with them.

To achieve this requires a spherical implosion, so maintaining the spherical symmetry is of utmost importance. This means that one must find a way to minimize the effect of the Raleigh Taylor instability, which is unavoidable, since ablative compression necessarily means the acceleration of a heavy fluid by a light one. An enormous effort has been made here, and the community generally agrees that the outward ablative flow has a strong stabilizing effect, although just how strong is still under study. In any case, by taking advantage of the flexibility one has in designing the laser pulse and target, one can exert a measure of control over the flow, so as to minimize the effect of the instability.

While Nuckoll's idea is still the main one being pursued today, as we will see, his original estimate of necessary laser energy was nothing if not optimistic. In the pursuit of laser fusion, LLNL (Lawrence Livermore National Laboratory) embarked on major program developing a series of larger and larger lasers, Argus, Shiva, Nova, Beamlet, and finally NIF. All of these are Nd glass lasers with a wavelength of 1.06 μm. However, at such long wavelengths, laser plasma instabilities become a major worry. Accordingly, LLNL has developed frequency multiplication techniques to operate at third harmonic, about 1/3 μm wavelength. LLNL now routinely operates with pulses in excess of a megajoule at third harmonic. URLLE has also taken this approach with their OMEGA laser (30 kJ). NRL has taken a different approach, using a KrF laser at a wavelength of 248 nm with its NIKE (3–5 kJ) and Electra lasers. More recently NRL has turned to shorter wavelength ArF lasers with a wavelength 193 nm.

In terms of economics and timelines, the experience of NIF has not been so different from the experience of ITER, but at a smaller scale. At least NIF is now operational. It was approved in 1995, to be finished in 2002 at a cost of $1.1B. It was finished in 2009 at a cost of $3.5B. It is also important to note that the sponsor for NIF is not fusion energy, but nuclear weapon stockpile stewardship. Accordingly, the sponsor has little interest in things important to energy such as laser efficiency, bandwidth, or rep rate. More important, the sponsor interest is only in a particular type of implosion driven by X-rays. This necessitated a particular type of target configuration called indirect drive. The target was placed inside a high Z enclosure called a hohlraum, the laser was focused on the inner walls of the hohlraum which heated to a temperature which produced black body X-rays at a temperature of 250–300 eV. These X-rays, not the laser, drive the target. The hohlraum is filled with helium gas to provide a back pressure to keep the heated walls from expanding into the target.

Once the laser light enters the hohlraum, the helium is ionized, so the light must traverse a large, likely nearly uniform plasma. Laser plasmas instabilities are a vitally important issue here, and LLNL has dedicated great resources to their analysis [46]. They believe they have things under control.

Furthermore, the sponsor, which paid for NIF, has many other uses for it besides fusion, and wants the facility for its own purposes more and more. A view of NIF, emphasizing the different important scale, kilometers down to millimeters is shown in Fig. 11.

Fig. 17

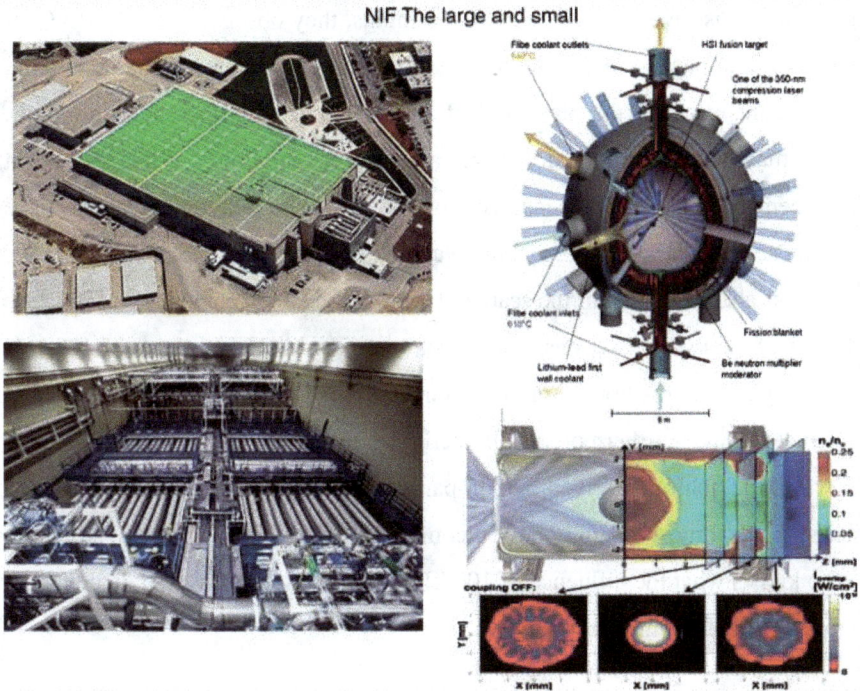

Figure 17 taken from the LLNL web site: Various photos of NIF, taken from the LLNL web site, emphasizing the tremendous range in size, from about half a kilometer for the overall facility, to the 100 m laser bays, to the 10 m target chamber, to the 1 cm hohlraum, to the 1 mm target.

In preparation for the ignition campaign, LLNL had done an enormous amount of theoretical work. In a major article [47], cited over 1500 times, Lindl and his coworkers have documented the theoretical basis for the project. A tremendous amount of work, by many people went into the preparation of this article; it is most likely beyond the capability of any single person to absorb all of it (certainly well beyond the capability of this author). However, the article is unambiguous in one respect, it predicts a Q (fusion energy over laser energy) of about 10 over a broad region of parameter space. As NIF was further delayed, LLNL's theoretical efforts continued. In another paper summarizing 6 years of additional effort [48], their predicted gain remained 10.

It is now well known that nature, at least initially did not cooperate. Their initial gains were just over 10^{-3}. Among other things, they observe about 10–15 % of the laser light back scattered out of the hohlraum by stimulated Raman scattering (a mechanism where the plasma electrons act collectively to scatter the light). There may be more scattered light remaining in the hohlraum. While this might not seem like a killer, one characteristic of stimulated Raman scatter in the nonlinear regime is that it generates copious energetic electrons, whose total energy is about half that of the scattered light. Hence, they could have as much as 100 kJ of energetic electrons, some with energies likely in excess of 100 keV bouncing around the hohlraum in a manner, which is likely nearly impossible to calculate today. Furthermore, in all likelihood there are 1–5 Megagauss magnetic fields in the hohlraum driven by non-parallel density and temperature gradients. These fields almost certainly have a complicated special and temporal structure. Who knows what the influence of 100 kJ of energetic electrons will be bouncing around the hohlraum will be.

Livermore continuously analyzed their results over a period of about a decade, with the Q gradually increasing. For the succeeding few years, the LLNL project has been inching up on what they define as a burning plasma, with this or that definition for their goal. As they advanced, they got Q's nearly as high as 10%. However, while they might have defined the plasma as burning, this depended on subtle interpretations of their measurement. Typically, they measured the neutron energy emitted, surmised the alpha particle energy produced (which was absorbed locally), and then calculated the PdV energy going into the fuel to heat it, and if it was less than the alpha energy, they claimed a burning plasma. Even with this only 'sort of convincing' justification for their claims, their paper describing these measurements (49) was downloaded over 80 *thousand* times (in this field ,a paper downloaded a thousand times is considered something of a classic)!

All that changed with their August 2021 shot. To their surprise (some of their diagnostics were set for lower fluxes and saturated!) and delight, they achieved 1.3 MJ of fusion energy from 1.7 MJ of laser light energy (50-52). Not only that, but they also achieved a non-subtle signature of a burning plasma. They measured the time dependent temperature of the exploding fuel after the 'bang time' when the laser was off, and saw that as it expanded, it *heated*. There is no other explanation for this other than alpha heating. They produced a burning plasma at least 15 years before ITER plans to if all goes well, and for a small fraction of the total cost of ITER. This was shown in an online seminar that they gave to the laser fusion community. This author attended.

They attempted to repeat the experiment, and as usual, they ran into trouble. For a year they could not do so. One of their scientists, Laurent Divol was invited to give a plenary talk at the APS-DPP (division of plasma physics) at the 2022 meeting in Spokane, Washington in late October (53). I heard his talk by listening remotely. Reading his abstract, most of it was about the trouble they were having because of the fill tube, asymmetries of the implosion, whatever. However, lightning stuck once again, just in the nick of time, and in early October, they had another successful shot, this one with a 1.9 MJ laser beam giving 1.2 MJ of fusion neutrons. Naturally, his talk was much different from what one might have surmised from only reading his abstract.

Finally, in December 2022, they had a shot in which the fusion energy was greater than the laser energy. About 2 MJ of laser energy produced ~3 MJ of fusion energy (54). The Secretary of Energy went to the lab to announce the achievement. Hence as of this writing (winter 2023), the lab has had 3 major shots, and there seems to be less and less time between these major successes. At the time of this writing, very little detail of these shots has been documented in the scientific literature, three scientific papers on the first shot (50-52) and none yet on the subsequent shots. The author takes great pleasure in being one of many to congratulate the Livermore lab on this phenomenal achievement.

To this author the major scientific advance is something which appeared in the two oral talks he heard but had not appeared yet in any of the written material he has seen so far. This is measurement of the temperature after the bang time when the laser is off. These measurements clearly showed the heating after the bang time, as the target expanded. These appeared only in the two talks which the author has heard (he has not been able to find these archived in several Google searches). Apparently, they have not been archived at the time of this writing, although undoubtedly, they will be archived in the scientific literature at some point soon. Hence the author includes his very rough hand drawn sketches (any errors are entirely the responsibility of the author, the LLNL lab had no part in providing these images).

In the September 2021 online seminar, one of the presenters showed a graph of the temperature, from the August 2021 shot, as a function of time after the bang. It looked something like that shown in Fig (18). In Laurent Divol's talk, he showed several two-dimensional images, at different times after the bang time, from the October 2022 shot. These are of a color-coded temperature at 3 times after the bang. The images looked something like that in Fig (18B). Each one clearly shows alpha heating, i.e. the formation of a propagating burn wave. To this author, these were the most spectacular results shown. LLNL claims to have by far the largest diagnostic capability for hot dense plasma; these images certainly support that claim.

Shot Aug, 2021, Laser energy 1.7 MJ, fusion energy 1.3MJ, Q=0.76! On line seminar, Sept 2021

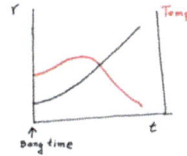

Shot Oct, 2022, Laser energy 1.9 MJ, fusion energy 1.2 MJ, Q=0.63! Laurent Divol, plenary talk DPP meeting.

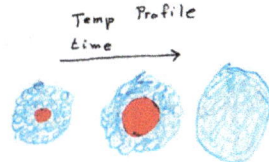

Figure 18: Images hand drawn by the author of the heating of the laser fusion target by alpha heating after the 'bang time'. These were from slides presented by LLNL personnel in seminars, and they show convincing evidence of the initiation of a thermonuclear burn wave.

Now that laser fusion is on the scoreboard, let's add up the score. While the results are nothing if not amazing and impressive, economic laser fusion power is hardly around the corner. Even with the Wright Brothers achievement, it took another half century to develop large jet powered aircraft. For one thing, while the maximum so far Q is 1.5, greater than the JET Q of 0.4, a more reasonable measurement for energy production is the efficiency of the driver η, times Q. For JET, η Q~0.1, while for η for the NIF is probably around 1%, so ηQ~0.015.

As noted earlier, the target in the LLNL experiment is inside a container called a hohlraum. Their laser is not focused on the target, but on the inner hohlraum walls, which emit X-rays which impinge on the target and implode it. As the goal of the project is nuclear stockpile stewardship, and not energy, the sponsor is only interested in X-ray drive and is not interested in things like efficiency, rep rate, or bandwidth, parameters important for energy. As the laser light does not directly strike the target, this configuration is called indirect drive. Figure (19), taken from Ref. (49) is a schematic of LLNL's configuration.

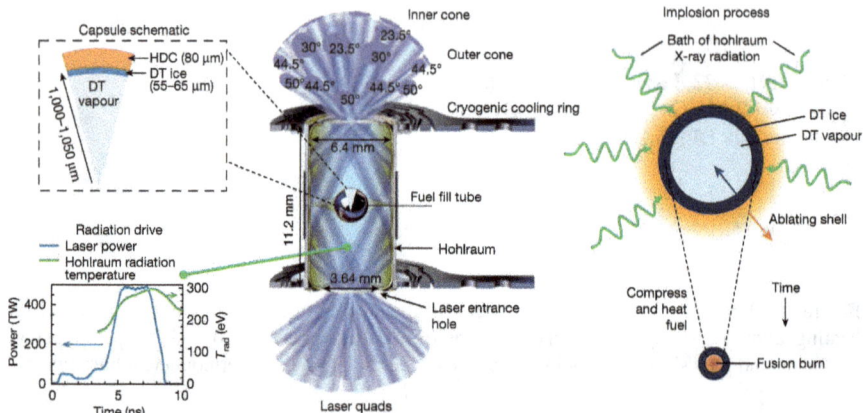

Figure (19): A schematic of the LLNL approach to laser fusion taken from Ref (49).

The path LLNL is on has quite a few problems if the goal is energy rather than nuclear stockpile stewardship. First of all, each shot involves a hohlraum, a precisely engineered container, made with expensive materials like gold or uranium and currently costing thousands of dollars each. While mass manufacturing of hohlraums will undoubtedly bring down their price considerably, even if the target produces a total energy of ~100MJ, which would translate to ~33MJ of electric energy, or ~ 10 kWhrs, worth about a dollar, it gives a very low-price limit for the ultimate economically acceptable hohlraum price. Second of all, only a small fraction of the laser light (in the form of X-rays) makes it to the target; the rest is lost through other channels. This is shown in Fig (20) taken from the LLNL publication (55).

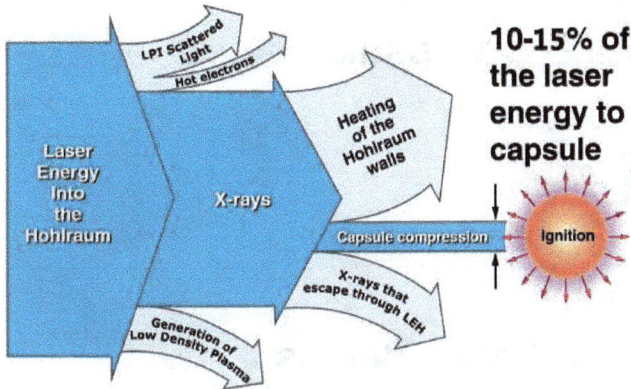

Figure (20): A schematic of where the laser energy goes for an indirect drive configuration. Only 10-15% of the laser energy makes it to the target in the form of X-rays. (55)

Finally, the LLNL configuration is fine for one shot, with the target on a small stalk, and focusing the laser on it is relatively simple. It is rather like hitting a golf ball on a tee. To do this continually, targets would have to be continuously shot in a high speed, with each shot certainly traveling in on a slightly different path. The target engagement becomes more like hitting a variety of Jacob DeGrom's fastballs, curve balls, sliders, changeups....., *on every pitch*. Not only does the target have to be in the right place, it has to have the proper orientation also, so the laser is aligned with the axis of the hohlraum, or to use the baseball analogy a bit further, the batter has to hit the ball at a precise phase of the ball's spin.

An alternative approach is what is called direct drive, where the laser light directly hits the target, without any of the losses specified in Fig (20). Figure (21) shows a schematic of direct drive configuration taken from NRL (56).

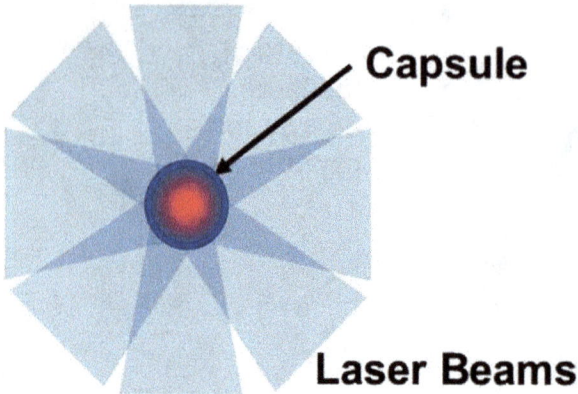

Capsule

Laser Beams

Figure (21): A schematic of direct drive laser fusion taken from NRL. The laser beams directly hit the target, so very little energy is wasted in other loss channels, as is the case with indirect drive. (56)

LLNL is not set up for uniform 4π illumination, but the University of Rochester Laboratory for Laser Energetic (URLLE) has done direct drive experiments with its smaller OMEGA (W) laser, with cryogenic DT targets [57]. While with their 30 kJ laser they could not achieve ignition they did get decent neutron production and central ion heating. Shown in Fig. 22, taken from (57) shows the neutron production and central ion temperature as a function of implosion velocity. The maximum neutron production is about 2×10^{13}, or about 45 J. Since the maximum energy of OMEGA is 30 kJ, this corresponds to a Q of at least 1.5×10^{-3}, not that much less that what NIF has achieved with on its initial indirect drive experiments.

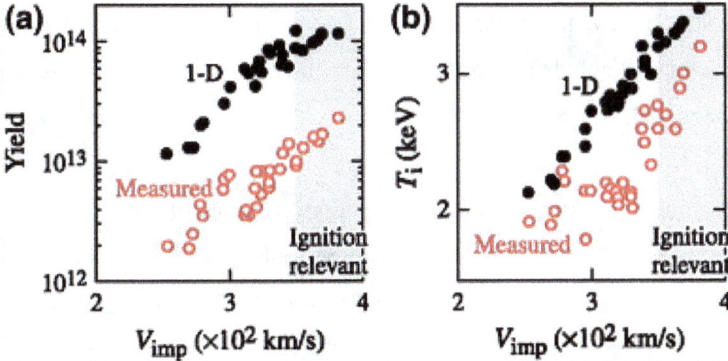

Figure (22): Measurements of neutron yield and ion temperature in direct drive powered by the OMEGA 30 kJ laser at URLLE. (57)

Since so much less laser light is wasted in direct drive, calculated gains (i.e.~ hundreds) are generally considerably higher than those gains calculated with indirect drive (i.e ~10) . NRL has done a number of calculations showing high gain (58-60) for a variety of target configurations and laser pulse structures. These are summarized in Fig. (23).

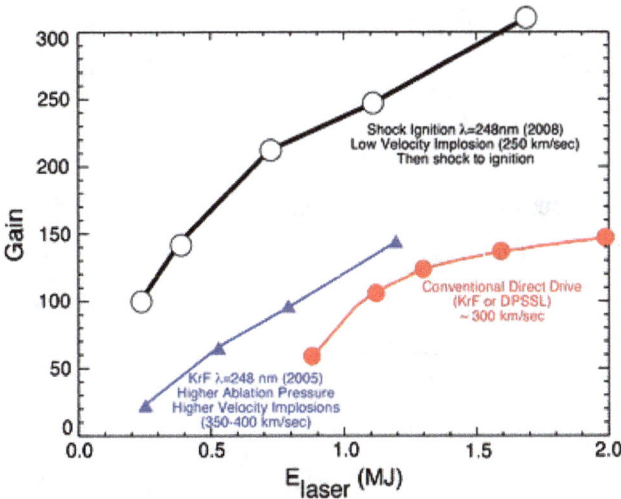

Figure (23): A variety of calculations of gain from NRL for direct drive laser fusion. (60)

Let us then set up two straw men for laser fusion. First say that one develops a 5% efficient, 1 MJ laser, and has a target with a gain of 100. This then gives

100MJ of fusion energy, translating to 33 MJ of electrical wall plug energy. However the laser will gobble up 20 of those MJ's just to run itself, so this would hardly be economical.

The second assumes a target gain of 200 and a laser efficiency of 10%. Here a 1 MJ laser would give 200 MJ or fusion energy per pulse, or 66 MJ of electric energy, and when 10 are subtracted to power the laser, 56 MJ of electric energy per pulse delivered to the grid. This would most likely be a viable power source. The device would have to operate at ~ 20 Hz to generate 1 GWe as a normal electric power plant.

But what does this mean for the development of economic laser fusion power this century, 78 years from this writing? First of all, one needs much more efficient high power lasers with greater bandwidth and rep rate. Then one has to illuminate a target and show that the gain calculation such as those in Fig (23) really do make sense. So far the best calculations have fallen far short in predicting gains (as pointed out, earlier LLNL estimates were 10, but it took them a decade to get to 1.5!)

Many of these issues were studied by a project, run by NRL, called HAPL (61) (High average power laser) which lasted about 10 years until it was cancelled in 2008. It was a multi institutional project which examined many such obstacles, including target manufacture, tracking, and engagement, final optics, laser development, target chamber, tritium production, recovering unburned tritium….

In the years of its existence, it made very good progress on many of the issues. For instance both NRL and LLNL developed preliminary versions of rep rated lasers which they saw as possible to develop into lasers relevant for laser fusion. Of course, given its short life time, HAPL had not completed the job. However it found no show stoppers. At least so far, there does not seem to be anything like tokamak conservative design rules, which greatly constrain what tokamaks can and cannot do, and pushes these reactors way up in size and cost.

More recently NRL has shifted its attention from KrF lasers to ArF lasers. Both are excimer lasers, KrF with a wavelength of 248 nm, and ArF with 193 nm. The shorter wavelength allows the laser light to penetrate more deeply into the target. It is also likely that the ArF laser will have the potential for higher efficiency, and greater bandwidth than KrF. Recently, on basically a shoe string budget, NRL set up an ArF laser with a pulse energy of 200 Joules. (62)

Assuming everything works as well as the HAPL project hoped and expected, can it all be accomplished, so that laser fusion power plants can be installed and become operational on a large scale before the end of the century? This author feels the answer is no. The job just seems too big and difficult. NIF took about half a decade longer to construct than was initially planned. The national ignition campaign (NIC) was to end in 2012 with a Q of ~10. Instead it took an additional decade to get a Q of 1.5. Already, past delays have gobbled up more than one and a half of the not quite 8 decades available, and the project still missed its original goal by nearly an order of magnitude.

Regarding the potential of economic laser fusion power in this century, this author is not bullish. Judging by the history up to now, this author's opinion is that there are just too many orders of magnitude to go, too many $$$ to get in support from uninterested sponsors, and too little time to get there, to reach economic power production and install it on a large scale this century. Obviously, many of us would make different predictions, but at this point I am sticking to mine. Of course, quoting Yogi once more, 'Predictions are tough, especially about the future'. Fortunately, or maybe not so fortunately, I am old enough so it is unlikely that I will see my prediction fail.

Since this section quoted Yogi Berra and mentioned Jacob deGrom, it seems appropriate, if only to lighten things up, to include an unnumbered image of Yogi from the USA postage stamp, and an image of a bobble head of Jacob deGrom from a visit to Citi Field to see a Mets game.

References

1. H. Kishimoto, S. Ishida, M. Kikuchi, H. Ninomiya
Advanced tokamak research on JT-60, Nucl. Fusion, 45 (8) (2005)

2. T. Luce, Realizing steady state tokamaks for fusion energy, Phys. Plasmas, 18, 030501 (2011)

3 S. Ishida, JT-60 Team, JFT-2M Group, High-beta steady-state research and future directions on the Japan atomic energy research Institute tokamak-60 upgrade and the Japan atomic energy research Institute fusion torus-2 modified, Phys. Plasmas, 11 (5) (2004), pp. 2532-2542

4. A. Isayamab, JT-60 Team, **Steady-state sustainment of high-β plas- mas through stability control in Japan atomic energy research Institute tokamak-60 upgrade,** Phys. Plasmas, 12 (Feb. 2005), p. 56117

5. P.B. Snyder, *et al.,* **High fusion performance in Super_H-mode experiments on Alcator C-Mod and DIII-D,** Nucl. Fusion, 59 (8) (2019)

6. R. Aymer**, The ITER project,** IEEE Trans. Plasma Sci., 25 (6) (Dec. 1997), pp. 1187-1195

7. D.J. Campbell, **The physics of the international thermonuclear experi- mental reactor FEAT,** Phys. Plasmas, 8 (5) (2001), pp. 2041-2049

8. www.iter.org

9. S. Ide, JT-60 team, Latest progress in steady state plasma research on the Japan atomic energy research Institute tokamak-60 upgrade, Phys. Plasmas, 7 (5) (2000), pp. 1927-1934

10. W. Manheimer, Hybrid fusion: the only viable development path for tokamaks? J. Fusion Energy, 28 (1) (2009), p. 60

11. W. Manheimer, Fusion breeding for mid-century sustainable power, J. Fusion Energy, 33 (3) (2014), pp. 199-234

12. W. Manheimer, Fusion Breeding for mid-century, sustainable, carbon free, power, Heliyon (Cell Network) Volume 6, Issue 9, September 2020, e04923, https://www.sciencedirect.com/science/article/pii/S2405844020317667#!

..13. W. Manheimer, Fusion Breeding and pure fusion development, perceptions and misperceptions, International Journal of Engineering and Applied Science, 202, Volume 7, p 125-154, https://www.ijeast.com/papers/125-154,%20Tesma0707.pdf

.. 14. J.P. Freidberg, F.J. Mangiarotti, and J. Mineervini, Designing a tokamak fusion reactor – How does plasma physics fit in, Phys. Plasmas, 2015, vol 22, number 7, p070901

..15. W. Manheimer, Magnetic fusion is tough – if not impossible – fusion breeding is much easier, Forum on Physics and Society, July 2021, published by the APS, https://higherlogicdownload.s3.amazonaws.com/APS/04c6f478-b2af-44c6-97f0-6857df5439a6/UploadedImages/P_S_JLY21.pdf

..16. F. Troyon and R. Gruber, A semi-empirical scaling law for beta limits in tokamaks, Phys. Letters 110A, 29, 1985

..17. F. Troyon et al, Beta limits in tokamaks and computational status, Phys. Plasmas, 30, 1597, 1988

.. 18. Harold Furth, John Kileen and Marshall Rosenbluth, Finite Resistive instabilities of a sheet pinch, Phys Fluids, 6, p 459, 1963

..19. H. Furth, P. Rutherford, and H. Selberg, Tearing modesin the cylindrical tokamak, Phys Fluids, 16, p 1054, 1973

..20. John Finn, Wallace Manheimer and Thomas Antonsen, Drift resistive interchange and tearing modes in cylindrical geometry, Phys Fluids, 26, p 963, 1983

..21. M Greenwald et al, A new look at density limits in tokamaks, Nucl, Fusion, 28, p 2199, 1988

..22. M. Greenwald, Density limits in tokamaks, Plasma Phys. Contr Fusion, 44, p27, 2002

..23. P. de Vries et al, Statistical analysis of disruptions in JET, Nucl. Fusion, 49, 055011, 2009

..24. N. Fisch and J. Rax, Interaction of energetic alpha particles with intense lower hybrid waves, Phys, Rev. Let. 69, 612, 1992

.. 25. W. Manheimer, Back to the future, the historical, scientific, naval and environmental case for fission fusion, Fusion Technol, 36, p1, 1999
..26. W. Manheimer, The scientific prototype, a proposed next step for the American MFE program, J. Fusion Energy, 32, 419-421, 2013

..27. W. Manheimer, Fusion breeding for midcentury sustainable power, Journal of Fusion Energy, 33, 199, 2014
https://link.springer.com/article/10.1007/s10894-014-9690-9

..28. W. Manheimer, Civilization needs sustainable energy – fusion breeding may be best, Journal of Sustainable Development, 15, p 98, 2022

.. 29. W. Manheimer, Fusion Breeding and pure fusion development, perceptions and misperceptions, International Journal of Engineering and Applied Science, 202, Volume 7, p 125-154,
https://www.ijeast.com/papers/125-154,%20Tesma0707.pdf

30. Schmidt, J. A. et al, *The Design of the Tokamak Physics Experiment (TPX)* Journal of Fusion Energy, 1993 12, 221

31. G. Giruzzi1 et al, *Investigation of steady-state tokamak issues by long pulse experiments on Tore Supra, Nucl. Fusion 2009 49 1*

32. Jong-Gu Kwak1et al, *An overview of KSTAR results, Nucl. Fusion* 2013 **53** 104005,

33. B.N. Wan, et al, *Overview of EAST experiments on the development of high-performance steady-state scenario*, Nuclear Fusion, 2017, 57, 102019,

34. Xiang Gao et al, *Recent results of fusion triple product on EAST tokamak, Plasma Sci. Technol.* 2021 **23** 092001

35. Another world record for China's EAST fusion reactor, Nuclear Engineering International, June 1, 2021

https://www.neimagazine.com/news/newsanother-world-record-for-chinas-east-fusion-reactor-8781515

36. D.J. Segall, A.J. Cerfon and J.P. Freidberg, *Steady state versus pulsed tokamak reactors*, Nucl. Fusion, 2021 **61** 045001

..37. L.E. Zakharov, What can and cannot be expected from tokamak fusion,, Atomic energy, 130, 2021 (Russian original,Vol 130, No2, Feb 2021)

..38. Gina McCarthy, White House meeting on fusion 'start ups' March 2022

https://www.whitehouse.gov/ostp/news-updates/2022/04/19/readout-of-thewhite-house- summit-on-developing-a-bold-decadal-vision-for-commercialfusion-energy/

39. A.J. Creely et al, Overview of the SPARC tokamak, J. Plasma Phys. (2020), vol. 86, 865860502,   Also see: Sorbon. B.N., et al., 2015, ARC: A compact, high-field, fusion nuclear science facility and demonstration power plant with demountable magnets,'' Fusion Eng. Des., 100, 378–405

40. .R.J. BUTTERY et al, The advanced tokamak path to a compact net electric fusion pilot plant, 2021, Nucl. Fusion, 61, 046028

41. WALLACE MANHEIMER, Comment on The advanced tokamak path to a compact net electric fusion pilot plant, Nucl Fusion, Volume 62, number 12, 2022

42.. J. Buttery et al 2022 Nucl. Fusion 62 128002, Reply to Comment on 'The advanced tokamak path to a compact net electric fusion pilot plant'

43. N. Rostoker, M. Binderbauer, and H. Monkhorst, Colliding beam fusion reactor, Science, 278, 1, 419 (1997).

44. .Martin Lampe and Wallace Manheimer, Comments on the Colliding Beam Fusion Reactor Proposed by Rostoker, Binderbauer and Monkhorst for Use with the p-11B Fusion Reaction, NRL Memorandum Report NRL/MR/6709--98-8305, October 1998

45. J. Nuckolls et al., Laser compression of matter to super high densities: thermonuclear (CTR) applications. Nature 239, 129 (1972)

46. R. Kirkwood et al., A review of laser-plasma interaction physics of indirect drive fusion. Plasma Physics and Con trolled Fusion **55**, 103001 (2013)

47. J. Lindl et al., The physics basis for ignition using indirect-drive targets on the National Ignition Facility. Phys. Plasmas **11**, 329 (2004)

48. S.W. Haan et al., Point design targets, specifications, and requirements for the 2010 ignition campaign on the National Ignition Facility. Phys. Plasmas 18, 051001 (2011)

49. A.B. Zylstra, O.A. Hurricane, D.A. Callahan, A.L.Kritcher, et al, Burning plasma achieved in inertial fusion, Nature, volume 601, pages 542–548 (2022)

50. A. B. Zylstra ,[1,*] A. L. Kritcher,[1] O. A. Hurricane,[1] D. A. Callahan, et al, Experimental achievement and signatures of ignition at the National Ignition Facility, Physical Review E 106, 025202 (2022)

52. A. L. Kritcher,[1,*] A. B. Zylstra,[1] D. A. Callahan,[1] O. A. Hurricane, Design of an inertial fusion experiment exceeding the Lawson criterion for ignition, Physical Review E 106, 025201 (2022)

52. H. Abu-Shawareb et al. Lawson Criterion for Ignition Exceeded in an Inertial Fusion Experiment, Physical Review Letters 129, 075001 (2022)

53. Laurent Divol, Plenary Talk, APS-DPP (division of plasma physics) meting, October 2022, Spokane, Washington

54. . https://www.llnl.gov/news/national-ignition-facility-achieves-fusion-ignition

55. Hybrid' Experiments Drive NIF Toward Ignition, https://lasers.llnl.gov/news/hybrid-experiments-drive-nif-toward-

56. https://www.nrl.navy.mil/News-Media/Images/igphoto/2002878402/

57. T. Sangster., et al., 2013 Improving cryogenic deuterium-tritium implosion performance on OMEGA. Phys. Plasmas **20**, 056317

58. S. Obenschain. et al., 2006, Pathway to a lower cost high repetition rate facility. Phys. Plasmas **13**, 05320

59. D. Colombant. et al., 2007, Direct drive laser target designs for sub megajoule energies. Phys. Plasmas **14**, 056317

60. A. Schmitt, A., 2010 et al., Shock ignition target designs for inertial fusion energy. Phys. Plasmas **17**, 042701

61. J.D. Sethian, et al, 2010, The Science and Technologies for Fusion Energy, IEEE Transactions on plasma science, Vol. 38, No. 4, April

V. Fusion breeding

Why fusion breeding?

As mentioned in the prologue, fusion breeding has always been the 'ugly duckling' for both the fusion and fission community. The fusion community takes pride in the fact that its source is perfect, no shortage of fuel, no intermediacy problem like solar and wind, no dangerous pollutants. In fact, while there is obviously no 'mass delusion' here (i.e. there is no mass), within at least in the APS and AIP, there are echoes of it. There are several APS and AIP journals where an article on fusion breeding would seem appropriate, and I have submitted probably half a dozen to different journals; they were all rejected at the 'opening the envelop' stage. It reminds one of the cancel cultures, no dissent will be allowed, which seems so prevalent in the scientific and media environment as regards climate change. Fortunately (for this author), other publishers of equal stature, Springer, the Cell network, and IEEE have been more than willing to publish such articles once properly reviewed. The author hopes that the grand pooh bahs of the APS and AIP become more tolerant not only to fusion breeding, which is a minor matter to most members, but especially to dissent on the climate issue.

But what is needed for human civilization? Remember the goal, at least as this author sees it, is to bring the entire world up to OEDC standards of prosperity by about midcentury. You might recall that we made the case that this means increasing power production from the current 14 TW (terawatts or trillion watts) to ~ 35-40 TW by midcentury, so all 10 billion of us can have a lifestyle like those in the OECD countries today. This book and many other dismiss out of hand windmills and solar panels with battery backup. Let's we do so by burning fossil fuel at 40 TW. First, we will likely be putting great stress on the fossil fuel supply.

Secondly, we will put CO_2 into the atmosphere 4 times faster than we do so today. The level would reach 800ppm well before century's end and keep increasing rapidly from that. While this author does not believe we are anywhere near a climate crisis at current use and atmospheric concentration of CO_2, better if we can keep the fossil fuel use to ~10 TW and worry about CO_2 in 200 or more years.

What about mined uranium? If Dan Meneley and George Stanford (see below) are right, and we run out of mined uranium, what then? Uranium from the oceans seems to be a pipe dream, and pure fusion, unlikely, at least for the 21st century and maybe more. In any case, it is certainly very, very risky to depend on either pure fusion or ocean based uranium. Hence, there are 3, and only 3 possibilities for worldwide sustainable energy not too long after midcentury, fast neutron fission breeding, thorium thermal breeders, and fusion breeding. Advocates of the first two are busy making their case; should the fusion effort just concede the field to them? This author thinks not. To this author it seems a no brainer. Not only is fusion breeding one of only three possibilities, more likely it is the best choice. Or as Patrick Moore wrote in an email to me in 2022: "Why has your pathway not been pursued, especially when the direct fusion approach has never produced what's needed?" Perhaps this effort can help to turn the ugly duckling into the beautiful swan.

What is fusion breeding

The 14 MeV fusion neutron does not only have to deposit its energy in the heat exchanger, it can also be used to convert a fertile nucleus (say ^{232}Th) to a fissile nucleus (^{233}U in this case). This fissile nucleus can be removed and burned in a separate thermal nuclear reactor. Alternatively, the fusion reactor can also burn this fissile nucleus, so that the reactor is actually some combination of a fusion and a fission reactor. Since the fissile nucleus releases ~ 200 MeV when it splits, as opposed to the 14 MeV fusion neutron, the amount of energy released, whether locally in the initial reactor, or in separate conventional thermal fission reactor can increase enormously. Either process is called hybrid fusion, or fusion fission. Only the former is called fusion breeding.

This author has researched, and advocated fusion breeding for over 20 years, and has published quite a few scientific articles on it over the decades, including several open access articles (1-5). References 1-4 are in established prestigious journals (but not APS or AIP). These articles also summarize the results from TFTR and JET with DT plasmas. Also there is a textbook chapter (6) and a brief summary in Forum on Physics and Society (7). These articles cite the early work which has not been published open access. They articles have made the case that fusion breeding is the only hybrid fusion that makes any sense. A fusion reactor is tough enough to develop, it does not need the added complication of a fission reactor inside. Furthermore, we have known how to make thermal fission reactors, which are reliable and safe for over 70 years. There is no need to combine it with fusion. In fact, if nuclear fuel were sustainably available, a competition between a fusion reactor and a fission reactor, say an LWR (light water reactor) is almost certainly unwinnable for the fusion reactor. However sustainable fuel from either mines or the sea is hardly a sure thing, in fact they are almost definitely *not* a sure thing. The relevant competition is between fusion breeding, fast neutron breeding, and thermal neutron thorium breeding.

But why go to fusion breeding, which is very tough to achieve? Why not just use fission breeding, which we basically know how to do? The answer is that fusion breeding, if we can pull it off, has enormous advantages over fission breeding. Whether the reaction is a fission or fusion reaction, each reaction produces 2–3 neutrons (in the fusion reaction this is after neutron multiplication, which is possible because the fusion neutron has a much higher energy than the fission neutron).

In fission, one of these neutrons is needed to continue the chain reaction and one is needed to replace the fuel atom; in fusion one is needed to breed the tritium from lithium, so in either case one or two neutrons are available for other purposes. Of course, in either case there are losses, so probably somewhere between half and one neutron per reaction is available for breeding 233U from 232Th, or 239Pu from 238U. However, the fission reaction produces about 200 MeV, while the DT fusion reaction produces only about 20. Hence for reactors of equal power, a fusion reactor generates about 10 times more neutrons, and therefore breeds about 10 times more nuclear fuel than a fission reactor does. Hence it takes two fission breeders to fuel a single thermal reactor of equal power at maximum breeding rate. However, due to the additional neutrons per reaction, and the lower energy of the fusion reaction, a fusion breeder can fuel 5-10 thermal reactors of equal power. In other words, a fusion reactor is neutron rich and energy poor, while a fission reaction is energy rich and neutron poor, a perfect match.

The next question is why go to fusion breeding, if one can do fusion, why not just do pure fusion? This does not have the additional complication of involving fissile or fertile materials, and one does not have to convince and partner with the nuclear industry, which might not even want us. The answer here is that fusion breeding is at least an order of magnitude to pull off than a pure fusion. If ITER and/or NIF are ultimately successful, one can rather easily envision transitioning the technology to commercial fusion breeders. However, to transition them to commercial pure fusion reactors would involve additional research which would take decades, and cost tens of billions of $$$; assuming it can be accomplished at all. Fusion breeding, likely is achievable, pure fusion might well turn out not to be. Even in a best-case scenario, where pure fusion does prove to be achievable, fusion breeding would provide an intermediate objective, of real economic value, decades earlier. At the very least it would be an important steppingstone to pure fusion, as well as a means of powering the world at 35-40 TW. As we have argued earlier, some sort of breeding will become essential, likely by mid-century. Fusion breeding very likely is the best option.

Fusion breeding is hardly a new idea. It is likely that the idea was originated by Andrei Sakharov in 1951 [8], although it may have in fact been earlier. Also, Hans Bethe argued for it in 1979 (9). These are two giants of 20th century physics; their analysis should have received much greater attention. Hybrid fusion was studied in the United States and other places in the late 1970's and early 1980's, but was then abandoned in favor of 'pure fusion', namely using only the kinetic energy of the fusion neutrons. Much of this information is archived in a web site [10]. This site contains many early LLNL (Lawrence Livermore National Lab) and PPPL (Princeton Plasma Physics Lab) reports, which would be difficult to access any other way. Generally, these reports considered a fusion device surrounded by a uranium or thorium blanket which provided a 'fission kick' to the power produced.

However, this 'fusion kick' does not only enormously complicate the reactor, but it is also not even necessary or advisable. For one thing, we have known how to build critical nuclear reactors safely for 70 years now, so once we have the fuel, why not burn it in the way we have always burned it.

In these earlier studies, fusion breeding, the use of fusion neutrons to breed nuclear fuel for other free-standing fission reactors was hardly ignored [11, 12, 13], but was certainly not emphasized either. This author sees the main justification for fusion breeding as combating a potential shortage of nuclear fuel. Furthermore, using fusion simply to breed fuel for stand-alone fission reactors fits in much better with current nuclear infrastructure, than does a fusion hybrid reactor, where every reactor is something very different from what is used at present. In short, it is not only possible, but likely, that fusion breeding could fill a pressing future need.

So, what has changed in the intervening 40 years to make it worthwhile to revisit the issue? Probably the main thing that has changed is that the predictions of fusion progress back then grossly underestimated the difficulty of the plasma physics task and overestimated the variety of potential plasma configurations. For instance, here is a quote from Bethe (9):

"Currently a large version (tokamak), the TFTR, is being built in Princeton: It will probably be completed in 1982 and may begin operation the following year. Its designers expect the Princeton tokamak to reach $Q \sim 1$".

Forty years after Bethe's article, this still has not happened! In fact, one of the main points of this book is that pure magnetic fusion is almost certainly too difficult, at least for providing economic power this century; fusion breeding most likely is not. The same is likely also true for inertial fusion. This alone seems to be a strong motivating factor for concentrating on fusion breeding instead of pure fusion

This author has been in email contact with two fission experts, Daniel Meneley (deceased 2018), who was once in charge of the Canadian program and worked on both the heavy water moderated CANDU (Canada Deuterium Uranium) reactor, and the Integral Fast Reactor (IFR), built by Argonne National Laboratory in the US. Earlier, he asserted in 2 separate emails [14]:

I've nearly finished prepping my talk for the CNS on June 13th (2006) -- from what I can see now, we will need A LOT of fissile isotopes if we want to fill in the petroleum-energy deficit that is coming upon us. Breeders cannot do it -- your competition will be enrichment of expensive uranium, electro-breeding. Good luck.

And:

We (I'm on the Executive Committee of the Environmental Sciences Division of ANS) held a "Sustainable Nuclear" double session at the ANS Annual in Reno a couple of weeks ago. I have copies of all the presentations. .... The result was an interesting mixture of "we have lots", just put the price up and we'll deliver (we've heard the same from Saudi recently) and "better be sure you have a long-term fuel supply contract before you build a new thermal reactor".

Another contact was with George Stanford (deceased 2013), a nuclear engineer and physicist who was a key member of the design team for the IFR. He wrote [15]:

Fissile material will be at a premium in 4 or 5 decades.....I think the role for fusion is the one you propose, namely as a breeder of fissile material if the time comes when the maximum IFR breeding rate is insufficient to meet demand.

Let us now consider the breeding of tritium. The conventional breeding reaction is usually assumed to be

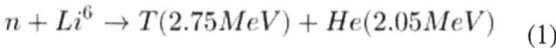

$$n + Li^6 \rightarrow T(2.75 MeV) + He(2.05 MeV) \quad (1)$$

This has the advantage of being exothermic, adding energy to the reaction, but the reaction costs a neutron. However if there are any neutron losses at all, an inevitability, the reaction will ultimately peter out. Even for pure fusion, a way must be found to produce additional neutrons. For fusion breeding, where more neutrons are required, the need is especially acute.

The key is that the fusion produces a much more energetic neutron, and an energetic neutron can produce more neutrons in particular targets. At an energy of 14 MeV, the neutron can produce several others (16), as is shown in Figure (1) for a lead target.

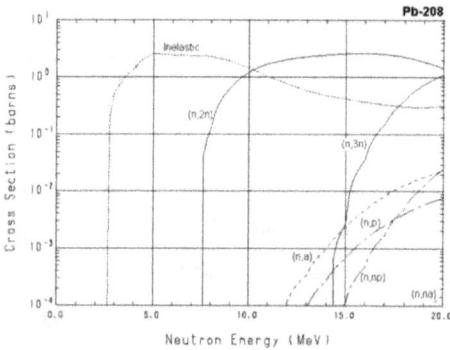

Figure (1). The cross sections for producing 1 or 2 additional neutrons in a lead target, as a function of the incident neutron energy. Taken from Ref. (16)

An even more prolific neutron source is beryllium, which requires a neutron energy of only 2.7 MeV to produce another neutron. Not only that, there is an additional tritium breeding reaction which conserves neutrons. It is

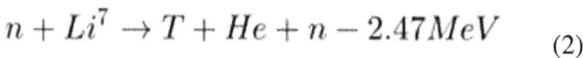

$$n + Li^7 \rightarrow T + He + n - 2.47 MeV \qquad (2)$$

This reaction is endothermic, and costs about 4.5 MeV as compared to the reaction in Eq. (3). However compared to the extra neutron, this energy loss is of no importance if the goal is fusion breeding. Let us say that after losses, the extra neutron breeds an extra half ^{233}U nucleus. When burned it produces ~ 100MeV, much more than making up for the extra energy needed to produce the extra neutron. In other words, the reaction in Eq.(1) gives a little more energy, while

176

that in Eq. (2) takes a little energy, but gives back *a lot* of energy.. Hence there are many possibilities for producing sufficient neutrons for breeding ^{233}U as well as tritium from the initial fusion reaction.

Each of these methods of breeding tritium begins with a fusion reactor. Hence if a fusion reactor exists, there is no problem in in breeding tritium to keep the process going. But now there are no fusion reactions, how does one get it all started? This author does not have a solution at this point, but there are several things to consider, which we will discuss briefly.

Most fission reactors use ordinary water as the moderator, and hence are called light water reactors or LWR's. One thing which limits the reactor is that the hydrogen in the water can also absorb a neutron, i.e. remove it from the reaction. In doing so the ordinary hydrogen becomes deuterium. However the CANDU reactors, pioneered by Canada, use deuterated water (i.e. D_2O) as the moderator. Their problem is that this deuterium also absorbs a neutron, but now becomes triton. At present there are ~ 40-50 CANDU reactors world wide; they generally have a stockpile of tritium on site and can be an initial source of it. It may become necessary for the world to build more CANDU's and fewer LWR's so as to produce more tritium. Furthermore, the nuclear powers all produce tritium for their nuclear deterrent, but of course little is known about this process, at least in the open literature. Wouldn't it be wonderful if the industries producing tritium for the big bombs, could use their expertise and convert it to an important peaceful purpose.

Of course fission plants cannot supply tritium for a fusion or fusion breeding based economy. The tritium is produced by a fission reaction givning ~200 MeV. However the fusion reaction it supports gives only 17.5 MeV. Obviously this does not add up. In any case, fission plants seem to be able to get the ball rolling.

In a steady state fusion economy, the tritium can be produced only from fusion. However because the fusion neutron has high energy, it can produce more than one tritium, probably at least 2 or 3, if that is the way the blanket is designed. Hence once there a few fusion reactors, their number can grow exponentially in time until there is a sufficient number to supply fuel for the world's thermal nuclear reactors.

Now let us consider the breeding process for ^{233}U. The collision cross section for both fission and neutron absorption for ^{235}U and ^{238}U is shown in Fig.(2) of the Section II. In general actinides with odd atomic mass have much larger fission cross sections at thermal energy, even atomic mass actinides do not. A fission breeder must work with the 2 MeV neutrons, while a thermal reactor burns neutrons with much greater reaction cross section. This renders a fast neutron reactor much more complicated, expensive, one which requires much more fissile material to get started, as well as exotic materials like liquid sodium and lead for coolants (at least exotic compared to water and air).

Now let us look at thorium - neutron reactions. When a neutron collides with a thorium nucleus, the absorption reaction has a cross section very much like uranium [3]. It goes from ^{232}Th to ^{233}Th. The new new nucleus is unstable, with a half life of about 20 minutes, to a single beta decay, where it becomes Protactinium, ^{233}Pa, which is itself unstable with a half life of about a month. ^{233}Pa beta decays and become ^{233}U, which is stable. However ^{233}U, having an odd number atomic weight has a large thermal neutron fission cross section, very much like that shown for ^{235}U. In other words it is fine as a fuel for thermal nuclear reactor. There is a similar reaction chain starting with ^{238}U and ending with ^{239}Pu, but since we would like to avoid plutonium to the extent possible, we do not consider this. Figure (2) is a schematic of the fusion based ^{233}U breeding process.

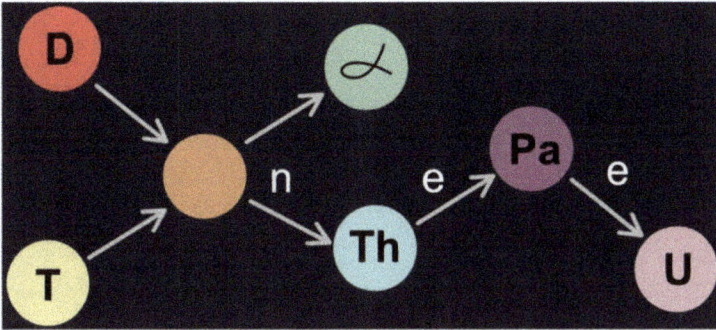

Figure 2: A schematic of the decay process where a fusion neutron is absorbed by a thorium nucleus, setting into motion a decay process which finally ends up as a ^{233}U nucleus; a perfectly good fuel for a thermal nuclear reactor.

It is important to note also that the reactions which take one from ^{232}Th to ^{233}U are exothermic, and roughly double the neutron power of the fusion reaction. To analyze the fate of a 14 MeV neutron entering a target, one uses Monte Carlo codes which all the main DoE labs have. Table 14.5 of Ref. (6) gives some examples of the energy released and the particles produced from a 14 MeV neutron entering particular homogeneous materials. A portion of that table is reduced as Table (1).

Medium	Product atoms	Energy released (Mev)
^{232}Th + 16% ^6Li	1.3 ^{233}U + 1.1 T	49
^9Be + 5% ^6Li	2.7 T	22

$^9Be + 5\% {}^{232}Th$	$2.66 \ {}^{233}U$	30
$^7Li + 0.8\% \ {}^{232}Th +$		
$.02\% \ {}^6Li$	$0.8 \ {}^{233}U + 1.1T$	17

TABLE (1) Product atoms and energy released by a 14 MeV neutron impinging on various homogeneous materials

Hence ITER, which is designed to produce ~ 500MW of fusion power, would, as a breeder, produce ~ 1GW; and the original Large ITER, designed to produce ~ 1.5GW, would, as a breeder produce ~ 3GW, about equivalent to a modern coal or nuclear powered electric generating plant. Many more details of the reactions as well as possible reactor designs are provided in Refs. (6 and 11-13). One design, using a realistic blanket geometry (12), would produce about 0.6 ^{233}U atoms, as well as the necessary tritium atom, from every 14 MeV neutron. However when burned, this produces ~120 MeV, multiplying the neutron energy by about an order of magnitude. Hence one breeder can fuel about 10 thermal reactors of equal neutron power, or about 5 of equal total power (recall the breeding reactions are exothermal and roughly double the the neutron total power).

Now let us do a very rough estimate of the cost of the fuel produced. This is based to a large degree on what the cost of an ITER scale reactor would be. Unfortunately, the cost of ITER has been increasing very rapidly, and not only is this discouraging, it makes an estimate difficult. The original cost of Large ITER was to be $10B in capital cost and $10B in operating cost for 10 years. Let us assume that the capital cost of the commercial prototype is $25B. The machine is assumed to last 30 years. Let us assume the same billion dollars per year operating cost.

Thus, as a very rough estimate, let us say the capital and operating cost of the commercial prototype is $2–2.5B/year. It both a breeder of ~ 15 GW of ^{233}U (i.e it produces ~ 5 tons of ^{233}U per year) and is a reactor, which generates 1GWe. Assuming it runs all year, and sells the power for ten cents per kWh, it earns about $0.9B. But it also produces 5 GWe of nuclear fuel. To recover the additional $1.1B, it would have to sell the nuclear fuel for about 2–3 cents per kWhr. This estimate is certainly not exact, and as capital and operating costs of ITER become clearer, it can be revised.

But at this point, the estimated cost does not seem to be any kind of showstopper. Uranium fuel for LWR's now costs about one half to one cent per kWh, so fusion bred fuel might increase the electricity cost by a penny or two per kWh.

To summarize, there does seem to be a roadmap to large scale, economic power production via magnetic fusion breeding by mid-century. Pure fusion can claim no such magnetic roadmap at this point. Pure inertial fusion might, as there are no conservative design rules that we know of holding it back. However, IFE still must get over significant hurdles to get the neutron production that MFE has right now. Unquestionably, fusion breeding is a more conservative goal for IFE than is pure fusion; perhaps it is the only reasonable goal.

There is one further complication, which is required for fusion breeding, which is not necessarily required for pure fusion. A pure fusion reactor might be able to operate with either a solid or liquid blanket if it can withstand the fusion environment. There are advantages and drawbacks to each. If the blanket is a solid, the tritium can be produced there can be extracted every year or two by replacing the blanket.

But a solid breeding blanket does not appear to be viable for fusion breeding. It not only breeds tritium, but also ^{233}U (or ^{239}Pu). In the neutron flux, these continue to react, producing a witches' brew of fission products, higher actinides, and an ever-increasing heat load. There is a real safety issue here. A major disruption would be a real disaster. Even for pure fusion with a solid blanket, the tritium in it decays with a half-life of 12 years. Waiting a year before claiming the tritium from the solid blanket, 8% of the tritium there at the beginning of the year would have decayed away and on the average, 4% would be gone in that year. Clearly even for pure fusion with a solid blanket a way must be devised to increase the tritium production.

The solution, especially for fusion breeding is to use a liquid blanket. It self-anneals and as the liquid with the tritium and ^{233}U or Pa flow out of the reactor region, these could be removed chemically as they are produced. The ^{233}U would then be mixed with ^{238}U to give a proliferation resistant fuel. Optimally, the liquid would have a free surface facing the plasma, but it is difficult to see how this can be designed in the complicated geometry of say a tokamak. However it could flow in pipes. These pipes would bring in some of the complications of a solid blanket, but if they could be inert to the flux of neutrons, radiation and fast ions or neutrals, it might be viable. They do not have to do anything but withstand the fusion environment. To this author, a liquid blanket seems overwhelmingly advantageous for pure fusion. For breeding ^{233}U, it is almost certainly a necessity.

If one has a liquid blanket, it does not seem to this author as if dissolving some U, Pa, or Th in the blanket will overly complicate the plasma facing parts, especially given that the neutron flux the blanket must accept is much lower for fusion breeding than for pure fusion. Of course, the chemical processing, to retrieve the T, ^{233}U or Pa, done away from the plasma will be much more complicated than retrieving T alone. However, this author assumes that it is a soluble, if difficult chemical engineering problem.

The web site, (10) has references to and links to several blanket designs for fusion breeding, including several old LLNL reports on the subject, which would be difficult to access in any other way. Also UCLA has a large program in blankets, studying many possible options (22).

Around the reactor there would be one or more regions of the blanket in which the lithium and thorium flow through the fusion neutron stream. They could either be pebbles carried along with a flow, or could be dissolved in the flow, most likely a molten salt. The salt FLiBe has been discussed for this purpose. Thorium, protactinium, and uranium are all soluble in it. The input to the flow has thorium and lithium dissolved, the output has some protactinium and tritium dissolved in it, and this is removed from the exiting fluid. A rough schematic, with the liquid flowing through pipes is shown Figure 3 . Here the lithium and thorium enter the blanket separately is shown in Figure taken from [11]. It is possible that a single pipe system could be used if the molten salt is FLiBe with thorium dissolved in it. Every element needed for the blanket would be included in the single fluid.

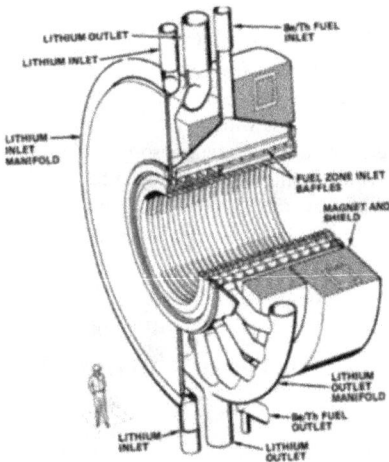

Figure 3: A schematic of a fusion breeding blanket surrounding a fusion reactor. Notice the input and exit pipes for the flowing lithium and thorium. (11)

It is also worth noting that laser fusion, which produces a point source of fusion products, opens up the possibility of of a liquid blanket with a free surface. One could use a segmented cylinder with liquid flowing down the sides, as shown in Figure (4).

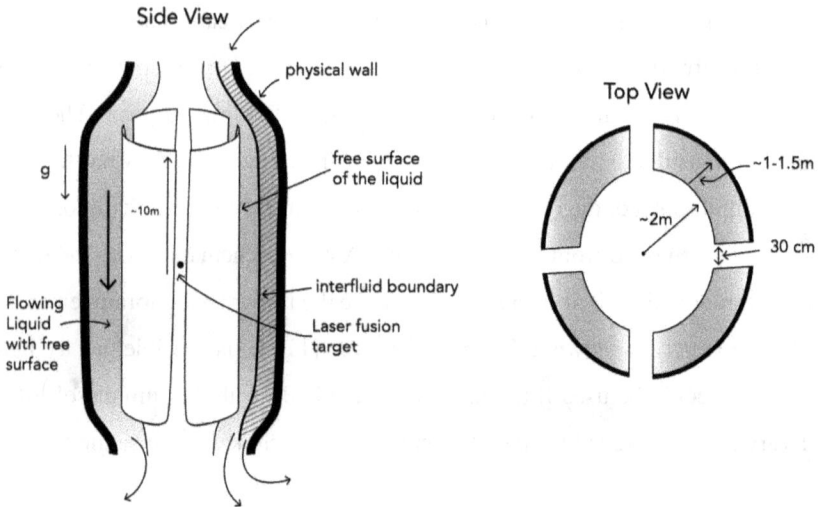

Figure 4: A schematic of a liquid blanket with a free surface flowing down a segmented cylinder. The side view is on the left. The flow going down the left-hand side of the cylinder is assumed to be a single fluid, on the right 2 fluids with no physical boundary between them. With the measurements shown here, the flowing liquid will absorb ~85% of anything emitted by the laser fusion target. With the 4 slots as shown and the open top and bottom, the laser could either be focused on the six faces of a cube, or on the 8 faces of an octahedron. The top view is on the right.

Preliminary development plans for achieving fusion breeding by mid century

In this section, we examine the potential routes to achieve economic fusion breeding not too long after midcentury. Unfortunately, the fusion community has confidence that they have a 'perfect' energy source for future civilization.

Hence right now, the main obstacle for the fusion community to get over is a psychological one. It should realize that fusion breeding is at least as good a goal, and possibly even a better one, than pure fusion. It is certainly one that it more achievable, likely not too long after midcentury, and by then, especially as the less developed parts of the world develop, it may be urgently needed.

Also, while there is a real need for mid and late century energy sources, there is no need to panic. If fusion breeding can come online in 30-50 years, that would be fine. Furthermore, it is a goal that fits in much better with current, and almost certainly the future, nuclear infrastructure. After all, it only must produce fuel for existing and future reactors. It does not have to set up an entirely new energy architecture, which historically has taken quite a few decades.

Perhaps George Stanford and Dan Meneley were right. Perhaps by mid-century the world will need a great deal more nuclear fuel than is available to continue to spread the widespread benefits of civilization. The top down approach to energy supply (Section II) certainly would indicate this. Not too long after midcentury, our descendants might be thanking us if we begin to develop fusion breading.

The rest of this section is divided into three parts. A. First it argues that laser fusion should be treated on (at least) an equal par with tokamak fusion. It presents a variety of arguments for this.

Then B, a possible development route for tokamaks, and C, a possible development route for lasers.

A. General discussion of inertial and magnetic fusion:

Here we argue for DoE in the USA to treat laser fusion on, at least an equal level, with tokamak fusion. This would mean, at the very least supporting several additional laser development programs and the related experimental work. Just as in the US there used to be several tokamaks, i.e., at PPPL, ORNL, GA, MIT,

185

Texas and UCLA, and now there is only one at GA, and it is not the largest; there should now be several well supported American laser development programs. If we do not build tokamaks, the rest of the world will, but at least right now, the US is the only ones with the potential to do laser fusion. Here we present some of the advantages we see for laser fusion as opposed to tokamak fusion.

1. Perhaps most worrisome, tokamaks still do not know how to drive the current, whether in a steady state or pulsed mode. The experiments for external current drive from EAST and KSTAR can drive the current externally, it just takes much too much power. Hopefully EAST, KSTAR and other superconducting tokamaks will find a way to externally drive the current at fusion relevant power The alternative seems to be an alternating current, but when the current passes through zero, there is no MHD equilibrium, and the plasma will immediately hit the wall.

2. Second, laser fusion is much safer. ITER will have a poloidal field and plasma, which we do not understand very well, and is subject to disruptions, with a stored energy comparable to a ~100-pound bomb. The superconducting magnet will have the energy of a ~1000-pound bomb. An uncontrolled quench, which happened at CERN a few years ago, would cause enormous damage. In CERN, it was in a miles long tunnel, so the damage was mostly local, but still took a year to repair. In the confined space of ITER, an uncontrolled quench would probably bring down the building and much more. The fusion breeding this work advocates only has small amounts of fertile material near the plasma at any one time. This fact alone certainly argues against putting a large amount of, say plutonium near the tokamak. Laser fusion does not store this kind of concentrated energy anywhere. For instance, NIF has 192 lasers, each of which has its own pulse power supply supplying perhaps a Megajoule. If one blows up, the damage will be localized and probably would not spread to others. A more efficient laser for a power plant would have even less stored energy.

3.MFE must worry about confining alphas, laser fusion does not. Experimentally, MFE is nowhere on this and probably won't be for more than a decade or two, until ITER starts producing them. Undoubtedly there are lots of paper studies on it. Laser fusion does not regard alphas as an afterthought. Alphas are built into the laser fusion culture at the ground level. Its entire rationale is to set up a burn wave, which NIF has already produced. MFE is nowhere near getting such a result. And once ITER does achieve a burning plasma, how will the heating be controlled? Do the alphas have to be removed? All of them? Some of them? Laser fusion does not have to tackle these very complicated issues.

4. Tokamaks, and any magnetic confinement scheme will always have to worry about recycling as 14 MeV neutrons, radiation, as well as fast ions and neutrals hit the wall and diverter plates. Who knows what is coming back and entering the plasma? In laser fusion, whatever hits the wall and bounces back, by the time it gets to the target, the fusion reaction will be long gone.

5. Tokamaks are constrained by conservative design rules (CDR's), meaning that any tokamak pure fusion device will be quite large. Most likely, in the light of CDR's, there is no way to shrink the size of the tokamak and still have it give enough power for pure fusion, and even a tokamak breeder will be quite large. At least as far as we are aware now, there are no such theoretical constraints on laser fusion. In fact an ICF burn wave has now been demonstrated at both the mega Joule and megaton level.

6. Laser fusion has flexibility in where it places the chamber wall, tokamaks do not. As we have seen in the last section, the use of a point source of fusion power opens up many different possibilities for the wall and blanket.

7. Laser fusion hardly has a clear glide path to commercial power development. It has to worry about developing an appropriate laser, laser efficiency, rep rate,

bandwidth, cost, target engagement and manufacture, final optics, target stability, ... These were all discussed in the HAPL program. To this author these various obstacles to laser fusion seem to be more technical in nature, whereas the obstacles tokamaks discussed above, seem to be more fundamental in nature. Tokamaks still need a huge international consortium, costing tens of billions to do in 15 more years (i.e. create a burning plasma), something which a laser has already done for a small fraction of the cost of ITER.

B. A plan to bring tokamak fusion breeding on line by ~ mid century

There are two immediate things the tokamak program should embrace.   First it should realize that if ITER is successful, large ITER probably would have been also. Counting the breeding reactions, it could be a 3GWth, 1GWe breeder which could fuel 5-10 thermal nuclear reactors of equal power, as discussed in the last section. ITER becomes an end in itself, not a means, on a long path to who knows what DEMO, to be put in place who knows how many decades later and for who knows how many additional $10's of billions, assuming it can be done at all.

Second, ITER should realize that it seems to have a serious problem with current generation. Possibly external current generation will ultimately be successful, but right now it takes too much power. A backup plan seems to be required, and probably the only reasonable backup plan is the use of an alternating Ohmically driven current.   In any case, this is a serious problem requiring ITER's full attention.

Something that ITER plans is to have are 6 ports, which 6 of the partners can use to explore tritium breeding (23). This author certainly recommends that at least one of these partners (preferably all in fact) use the ^{7}Li pathway to breed the tritium. This way they preserver the neutron for other applications, not only for breeding fissile fuel, but also for breeding sufficient tritium to make up for losses.

Perhaps one or more of the partners could also use their particular port to produce some ^{233}U on a small scale. This way the fusion project would produce something, admittedly on a very small scale, that the world could actually use.

Hence ITER should continue pretty much on the path it is on, with consideration given to the two points above. It should not expend any further resources on the DEMO, which probably will never become an economical power supply and almost certainly will never be built. Instead is should dust off its plans for Large ITER, but alter them so that it could be used with a flowing blanket, probably a molten salt. Then it would be ready for construction assuming ITER is successful. Likely, if ITER could also solve the current problem, the world would be ready to seriously begin implementing fusion breeding on a large scale.

There is also a great deal that can be accomplished with smaller tokamak experiments. For decades this author has argued that the tokamak program in the United States should build a tokamak he called 'The Scientific Prototype'. This is a tokamak about the size of TFTR, JET or JT-60, 2 of which have already produced large numbers of 14 MeV neutrons. The idea of the scientific prototype was to reproduce this in steady state, or at high duty factor, in a DT plasma, and also to breed its own tritium and to recover its unburned tritium for reinsertion into the plasma. In fact, JET has already at least made a start on recovering unburned tritium [24]. If the scientific prototype were built, and was successful, it would have given crucial high duty cycle data; ITER, if successful, would give Q~10 data. If both were successful, the world could embark on a tokamak based fusion breeder program, decades before pure fusion could be ready, assuming it could ever be ready at all.

Unfortunately the DoE did not adopt this path, and neither did PPPL. Had PPPL instead adopted the scientific prototype between say 2000 and 2010, by now it would surely have confronted the current drive problem, and perhaps would have solve it one way of another. By the time ITER had completed its job on a pulsed machine, a tremendous amount would have already been learned on steady state or high duty cycle operation. In a worst case scenario, it could have alerted ITER to the fact that steady state or high duty cycle operation of a tokamak had serious unresolved issues. Perhaps it is still not too late to build the scientific prototype, if not in the US, perhaps somewhere else in the world.

Most of this author's advocacy of the scientific prototype assumed external current drive. However on becoming aware of the discouraging EAST and KSTAR result, his most recent efforts (5) have explored an oscillating Ohmically driven current. The goal was to start with a duty cycle of ~20% and work up to ~80%. Perhaps there is something to this approach.

At this point, unlike France, China, and Korea, the US has no superconducting tokamak. However it looks like we will soon have one by Commonwealth Fusion, one that can operate at any magnetic field between 3 and 12T. Perhaps once its tokamak becomes operational, Commonwealth Fusion should shift its priorities to solving the steady state current drive problem, either by external drive at an acceptable power, or by an oscillating Ohmically driven current, or by some other means they devise. They will not be giving their investors the pilot plant they promised, but they will not be giving them this pilot plant, in a decade, no matter what they do. Rather than spending the next decade tilting windmills, perhaps they should use their expertise to solve a real and immediate problem in tokamak fusion, namely finding an acceptable way to drive the current. If successful, this would be a genuine and vital contribution they could make in the next decade. They seem to have the equipment and expertise to tackle it as well as anyone else, at least anyone else in the US.

C. A plan to bring laser fusion breeding on line by ~ mid century

While this paper is optimistic as regards laser fusion, especially for breeding, there is little eperimental evidence, or plans, to suggest which way to go. In the last section, it was shown that while a 10% efficient laser with target gain of 200 would be fine for pure fusion, a 5% efficient laser with a target gain of 100 would not.

What is vital is to set up experimental and development laser and target programs to see what is feasible and what is not. This author here proposes a three pronged attack on laser and target development. Two of these prongs were proposed by Steven Bodner in a letter to the National Academy of Science, a letter that should have received much more attention than it did. Figure (6) shows a schematic, taken from (25) showing the plan regarding both laser development, as well as the target and chamber design.

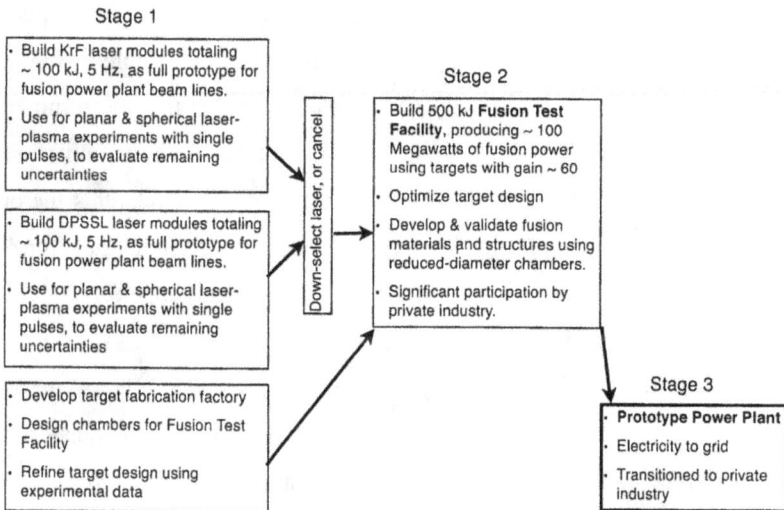

Figure (5): Steven Bodner's proposed plan for laser development for laser fusion. (25)

While this author basically agrees with Bodner's plan there are several areas where he does not. Let's consider first Stage 1. In the intervening years, NRL has shifted its emphasis to ArF lasers. These radiate at 193 nm wavelength instead of the KrF laser's 248 nm, giving significant advantages to the laser target interaction. On a shoe string budget, NRL has shown that these operate well at the two hundred Joule level, while their KrF lasers have long been demonstrated to operate well at the multi kilo Joule level.

Secondly, Bodner's plan, at the transition from stage one to stage two has some tough transition criteria, too tough in this author's opinion. First of all, say ArF reaches that milestone first. Does that really mean that DPSSL lasers should just be immediately abandoned, or visa versa? Perhaps further research, at lower level, by the temporary loser could still develop to a superior product. Secondly if neither of the lasers reach the required level for transition to stage 2 by some deadline, should the whole project be abandoned?

To this author, neither of these hard end points make any sense. The entire history of the fusion projects is one of both substantial progress, but coupled with large cost overruns and delays. Is it really reasonable to demand that these suddenly stop now, and expect all progress to be made strictly according to some initial budget and time line, or else? This author thinks not. He thinks that the only reason for such an abrupt end for laser fusion should be if the tokamak project forges so far ahead that pursuing laser fusion can no longer compete.

As argued in Section II, this energy development program is of extreme importance for the continuation of modern civilization. While obviously every effort should be made to develop the many parts of it as rapidly and as economically as possible, it should not be held strictly to any schedule or budget. It is a very difficult, but vitally important project. It is not easy to predict its ultimate cost or schedule. If it is delayed, there will still be plenty of fossil and nuclear fuel to get us through a decade or two. If it costs a couple of $$B more, it is not the end of the world. After all, the world can currently afford hundreds of billions of $$$ per year, with hope to increase this to more than ten trillion per year, for wind and solar, which will never lead to economical, reliable, and environmentally suitable power. Hence, if it proves necessary, it can surely afford a few billion per year more for fusion and/or fusion breeding, which has a real chance of working.

The third leg of the laser development plan is obvious. Since LLNL has made such an important leap, and has a mega Joule laser right now, its work obviously should be continued. Also it has a huge infrastructure in place, one which would not be possible to rapidly duplicate anywhere else.   Look at the photos of the participants of HAPL meetings. There were ~ 50-100 people. Then look at the picture LLNL NIF group shown in their September 2021 zoom seminars. There were ~ 500-1000 people in the picture. They are certainly the giant, the elephant in the room. They have an enormous infrastructure already in place. If LLNL gets to the point where it is able to produce burning plasmas frequently and reliably, it could have a big impact whether the ultimate machine turns out to be a tokamak or laser. For instance it could begin experimental studies of breeding tritium and ^{233}U, and also begin studies of recapturing unburned tritium.

With its Q = 1.5 result, LLNL is obviously on a roll, it should continue along the present track, but not for that much longer. Probably in a year or two, it will achieve a larger Q, maybe even 3, or 4 and if they achieve this, once again it will be a spectacular achievement. However where the goal becomes energy, it has no choice ultimately, but to shift away from indirect drive to direct drive. Indirect drive, just puts too much laser energy everywhere but the target.

But first let us briefly discuss an intermediate option. The URLLE group has done a considerable amount of work on what they call polar direct drive (26).   This uses the optics basically as they are, but modified for direct drive, so that the illumination is mostly at the poles and is not spherically uniform. URLLE thinks that it can partially make up for the lack of spherical illumination in other ways. Both Bodner and this author are skeptical of polar direct drive. Here is Bodner: (25)

Their polar direct drive proposal is feasible, but there are uncertainties and it is premature to evaluate their chance of success.

Here is the author from his 2014 paper (1)

This author worries that polar direct drive could be a large time and dollar sink spent on a non-optimum configuration.

This author believes a viable alternative is to convert NIF to direct drive illumination. Bodner argues against this for several reasons. He first states:

Unofficial and rumored estimates from LLNL say that the conversion to symmetric illumination for direct drive would cost over $300 M and take at least 2 years. Since the paying customer is the weapons program, it won't happen.

Then he also argues that the laser is not good for direct drive for a variety of reasons, including insufficient bandwidth, non-optimum optical smoothing, etc. As Bodner put it:

No one in the direct drive program would have voluntarily chosen a NIF-type laser to test their target designs.

To consider these objections one by one, first, priorities do change during a project. When NIF was built, the priority was stockpile stewardship. Now it should certainly be energy; some things will have to change. Furthermore, the weapons program will have had the laser and target in their desired configuration for 15 years. Now it time for a change to a direct drive configuration, which is optimal for energy; and anyway, who says that even in a direct drive configuration NIF cannot still have important applications for the weapons program.

Bodner's phase one would use lasers that are of the type much more optimal for laser fusion, but they would be 'only' 100 kJ. But if we have another mega Joule laser just sitting around, shouldn't we use it, even if it is not ideal? Bodner apparently thinks not. This author thinks we should. Furthermore, URLLE believes that they can get decent results using a polar direct drive configuration with NIF. Surely, they must believe they can do better with uniform 4π illumination. Livermore achieved a burning plasma with only ~ 10% of the laser energy absorbed by the target. Surely it must think that getting 80-90% on target at least might well improve things. Even a very sub optimal implosion from NIF in a direct drive configuration, would teach us great deal about burning plasmas, information that could be useful not only for the laser program, but also for ITER.

As in the author's 2014 paper [red, for hindsight, is added today]:

"Also, direct drive gain calculations show impressive gains at half a megajoule laser energy. NIF has nearly 4 times this. Hence there is a very large margin for error both regarding the laser energy and the gain calculations. Let's say NIF does a symmetric direct drive experiment and gets a gain of 'only' 10. (with the benefit of hindsight, I would have said 'only' 3 or 4.) Wouldn't this be a tremendous accomplishment? It might be just 2 or 3 years away."

Here is Bodner on how to design the target and laser:

Design both the fusion target and the laser with significant safety features. Then if there are surprises, one can recover.

These seems to say that even with a non-ideal 1 MJ laser, there is a very significant amount that can be learned from implosion experiments with NIF in a direct drive configuration. These 3 legs for the laser development seem to this author to be a reasonable plan for developing fusion breeding via laser fusion by midcentury. But now let us consider what comes next. Bodner's phase 2 is the use of a 500 kJ laser to achieve a gain of 60. Then the goal would be to go on to phase 3 with a much higher gain and higher laser efficiency.

But to achieve commercial fusion breeding, a somewhat modified phase 2 might be all that is needed. There might well be no need for his phase 3, if fusion breeding is the goal. The laser with a gain of 60 and an efficiency of 5% would almost certainly be fine for laser fusion breeding.

So instead of a 500 kJ laser for phase 2, let us consider a 1 MJ laser which satisfies all of Bodner's phase 2's requirements. This seems reasonable, after all, we have a 1 MJ laser right now, but we do not have a target design which we can say with any confidence will have a gain of anywhere near 60. This would (hopefully) be accomplished in phase 2. So, at the end of phase 2, we would expect to have a 1 MJ laser and a target with a gain of 60 to produced 60 MJ of output fusion energy. However, used as a breeder, this 60 MJ of fusion neutron energy means 600 MJ of fuel, plus another 60 MJ of energy from the breeding of ^{233}U. Now say this runs with a 20 Hz rep rate. This means it would produce 12,000 MW of nuclear fuel, enough to fuel four 1 GWe LWR's and also supply 400 MWe to the grid.

In other words, using fusion breeding as a goal, rather than pure fusion, the laser fusion program can skip Bodner's phase 3, and use a successful, modified phase 2 to go right to commercial power and fuel production.

What if a viable pure fusion device suddenly becomes available?

Let's say that somehow a viable pure fusion device becomes available, let's say a tokamak with a 3-meter major radius, which produces 3 GWth of 14 MeV neutrons. This obviously violates CDR's by a large margin. Not only that, it puts a very large neutron loading on the wall. But let's stipulate it anyway. Let's also stipulate that it needs only 30 MW of input power, small enough that we, so we can forget about it in our calculations. Then run through a conventional heat exchanger, it produces 1 GWe. Let's say the device only costs $4B and lasts for 30 years, or costs ~ $130M per year. Let's say that interest is another $130M, recapitalization over the 30 years costs another $100M, and operating expenses are $500M per year for a total cost of $860M per year. This means it costs $0.1 per kWhr to produce, so let's say it sells the power for 12 cents per kWhr. This could be a successful use for fusion.

Is this the end of the story for fusion breeding? Probably not! First of all, such a tokamak is most likely not possible. However, let us see what this it can do as a fusion breeder. Here we consider a blanket not mainly to exchange the heat generated by the 14 MeV neutrons, but to maximize additional neutron production. First breed the tritium using the ^{7}Li reaction. This takes about 3 MeV from the fusion neutron, but does preserve a neutron. The fusion neutron now has ~ 11 MeV. Then consider a second blanket of mostly beryllium. It can generate additional neutrons at an energy cost of ~ 3 MeV per neutron. Thus we may be able to generate as many as 3 additional neutrons from the 11 MeV neutron after it has produced the tritium atom, making 4 neutrons all together. Let's say that half of these neutrons are used to generate ^{233}U atoms and the half are lost due to various loss mechanisms. Hence each 14 MeV neutron could ultimately generate two ^{233}U fuel atoms producing a total of ~ 400 MeV when burned. This reactor with the enhanced breeding blanket, could fuel as many as

197

25-40 one GWe reactors at a fuel ~0.2 cents per kWhr, almost certainly cheaper than mined uranium will be then. While electricity will not become 'too cheap too meter', at least the fuel will be.

So how would society use this reactor; as a power source, or as a breeder? Clearly, it is impossible to know, this not a decision for us to make, but for our children and grandchildren. This author's guess, but only a guess, is that a breeder would be a better choice. The point is that planning for a breeder now, with reactors which seem to be decent breeders, but not viable for pure fusion, we do no harm, but do only good. If now we can foresee only such breeders, as is the reality today, they will be a huge benefit to society. However, if by some miracle, we see how to build an economic pure fusion reactor, it will be an even better, cheaper breeder. Society will be able to make a choice as to which path it would like to follow.

The energy park

Since 2004, every article the author has written on fusion breeding has ended with a section on 'The Energy Park', and this is no different. The energy park is a proposed key element of an energy infrastructure to supply tens of terawatts to the world. It uses the fact that a fusion breeder can breed fuel for at least 5 LWR's of equal power, and each year an LWR discharges about 1/5 of its fuel as plutonium and higher actinide (17).

The energy park proposes to burn the discharged actinides with a fast neutron reactor like the IFR. This is different from the French approach, which recycles these actinides to fuel for thermal reactors. But the thermal reactor also creates additional actinides, of constantly higher atomic number, and as the process is repeated, produces a more and more complicated stew of nuclear wastes. The advantage of fast neutron reactor is that one time through, it burns all actinides as they all have about the same reaction cross section. There is no endless recycling, a single burn will take care of all the actinides.

This series of papers have invariably assumed that the waste products of the thermal reactors must be rendered harmless. The alternative is burying them somewhere and creating what amounts to a 'plutonium mine', which will plague society for half a million years or so. This is an immoral burden to lay upon our descendants, hence the need for the fast reactor in the energy park.

One envisions an energy infrastructure where there is one fusion breeder to supply fuel to about 5 thermal reactors like the LWR or CANDU or more advanced reactor, and one fast neutron reactor to burn the 'waste' actinides.
The fast neutron reactor could be something like the Integral Fast Reactor (IFR), developed by Argonne National Laboratory. It ran successfully at 60 MW for years before it was disassembled. It could run on any actinide and could run in

either a breeder or burner mode. As we see in Fig (2) from Section I, at ~1-2 MeV neutron energy, fissile and fertile materials have about the same fission cross sections. Thus, the IFR can be run in a mode to simply 'burn' any actinide. Specifically, it could be used to burn all the plutonium and other higher actinides that an LWR discharges.

The British, who have the largest plutonium 'waste' stockpile, are now seriously considering constructing a much larger version of the IFR called PRISM to 'treat' their large stockpile of plutonium waste. Perhaps they are making an important step in the ultimate development of the energy park.

A schematic of the energy park is shown in Figure (6). Most of the elements of the energy park are available today, only the fusion breeder needs full development.

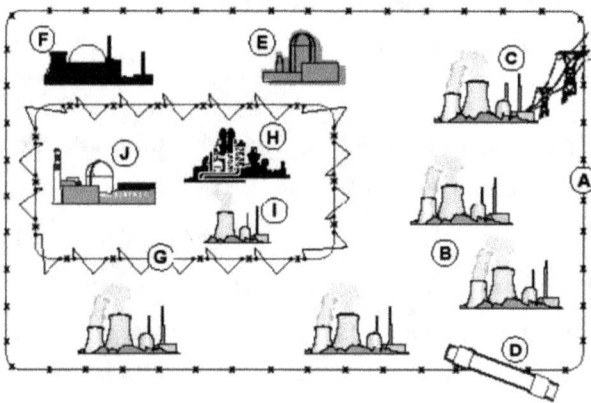

Figure 6: The energy park: A. low security fence; B. 5 thermal 1GWe nuclear reactors, LWRs or more advanced reactors; C. output electricity; D. manufactured fuel pipeline, E. cooling pool for storage of highly radioactive fission products for 300–500 years necessary for them to become inert. This is a time human society can reasonably plan for, unlike the ~ half million years it would take for the plutonium 'waste' to be buried in a repository, essentially creating a plutonium mine; F. liquid or gaseous fuel factory; G. high security fence, everything with proliferation risk, during the short time before it is diluted or burned, is behind this high security fence; H. separation plant. This separates the material discharged from the reactors (B) into

fission products and transuranic elements. Fission products which have commercial value would be separated out and sold, the rest go to storage (E), transuranic elements go to (I); the 1GWe integral fast reactor (IFR) or other fast neutron reactor where actinides like plutonium are burned; J. the fusion breeder, producing 1GWe itself and also producing the fuel (ultimately enriched to ~4% ^{233}U in ^{238}U) for the 5 thermal nuclear reactors for a total of 7 GWe produced in the energy park.

The world-wide use of energy parks could generate carbon free power, in an economically and environmentally viable way, and with little or no proliferation risk. They could supply tens of TW at least as far into the future as the dawn of civilization was in the past.

References

1. Wallace Manheimer, 2014, *"Fusion breeding for mid-century sustainable power,"* J. Fusion Energy, , 33, 199–234,. [Online]. Available: https://link.springer.com/article/10.1007/s10894-014-9690-9

2. Wallace Manheimer, 2018, *Midcentury carbon free sustainable energy development based on fusion breeding*, IEEE Access, December, Vol 6, issue 1, p 64954-64969, https://ieeexplore.ieee.org/document/8502757

3. Wallace Manheimer 2020, *Fusion breeding for mid-century, sustainable carbon free power, Helioyon (Cell network)* #1 6 e04923 https://www.sciencedirect.com/science/article/pii/S2405844020317667#!

4. Wallace Manheimer, 2020, *Fusion breeding as an approach to sustainable energy.* Discover Sustainability 1, #2. https://doi.org/10.1007/s43621-020-00004-9

5. Wallace Manheimer, *Fusion breeding and pure fusion development perceptions and misperceptions,* International Journal of Engineering, Applied Science and Technology, 2022, Volume 7, https://www.ijeast.com/current-issue.php , p 125-154, also see: http://arxiv.org/abs/2212.00907, Dec 1, 2022

6. Ralph Moir, Wallace Manheimer, 2013 , *Hybrid Fusion, Chapter 14 in Magnetic Fusion Technology, by Thomas Dolan* (Springer, New York,)

7. Wallace Manheimer, 2021, *Magnetic fusion is tough- if not impossible- fusion breeding is much easier,* Forum of Physics and Society, July, #1, APS publication https://higherlogicdownload.s3.amazonaws.com/APS/04c6f478-b2af-44c6-97f0-6857df5439a6/UploadedImages/P_S_JLY21.pdf

8. Andrei Sakharov*Memoirs* (Vintage Books, New York, 1990), p. 142

9. H. Bethe, *The Fusion Hybrid, Physics Today* (May 1979)

10. www.ralphmoir.com

11. R.W. Moir, J.D. Lee, M.S. Coops, *Fission-suppressed Hybrid Reactor: the Fusion Breeder*, Lawrence Livermore Nat. Lab., Liver- more, CA, USA (1982) LLNL Rep. UCSD 19638 [Online]. Available: https://www.ralphmoir.com

12. R.W. Moir, *The fusion breeder,* J. Fusion Energy, 2 (Oct. 1982), pp. 351-367

13. R.W. Moir, *Fission-suppressed fusion breeder on the thorium cycle and nonproliferation,* Proc. AIP Conf., vol. 1442 (2012), p. 346

14. Dan Meneley, private communication 2006

15. George Stanford, private communication 2006

16. . National Nuclear data center https://www.nndc.bnl.gov/sigma/index.jsp This web site has a large amount of nuclear data

17. Richard Garwin and George Charpak., 2001 *Megawatts and Megatons* (Knopf, Distributed by Random House, New York,)

18. Y. Chang. 2002, *Advanced fast reactor: a next generation nuclear energy concept.* Forum Phys. Soc.

19. W, Hannum., W, Marsh. and G. Stanford., *Purex and Pyro are not the Same* (Physics and Society, vol 32,) 2004,

20. T. Beynon. et al., *The technology of the integral fast reactor and its associated fuel cycle.* Prog. Nucl. Energy **31**(1/2) 1997

21. L. Freeman., *et al., "Physics experiments and lifetime performance of the light water breeder reactor," Nucl. Sci. Eng.*, vol. 102, pp. 341–364, Aug.. 1989

22. www.fusion.ucla.edu/abdou

23. Arnoux R. 2016 *Tritium: Changing Lead into Gold* (ITER Magazine) (https://iter.org/mag/8/56)

24. Peacock A.T., Andrew P.A., Brennan D., Coad J.P., Hemmerich H., Knipe S., Penzhorn R.-D. and Pick M. 2000 Tritium inventory in the first wall of JET *Fusion Eng. Des.* 49-50, November 2000, p 745-752

25. Steven Bodner 2011, Letter to Members of the National Academy of Sciences Committee on the Prospects for Inertial Confinement Fusion Energy Systems, and the Panel on Fusion Target Physics, December 9, (available from the author and other sources)

26. R.S.Craxton., et al, Polar direct drive: Proof-of-principle experiments on OMEGA and prospects for ignition on the National Ignition Facility, Physics of Plasmas **12**, 056304, 2005

Epilogue

The real problem the world faces is not climate change, it is lack of suffcient energy for the developing parts of the world. In this age of instantaneous communication, how much longer will a world with a percapita power use of 5 kW for OECD countries, and 1 kW per capita for the rest of the world be acceptable and sustainable? But to bring the rest of the word up to OECD standards by midcentury would require about tripling the rate of power increase above what BP predicts will happen. At this point, despite inspiring, no pious lectures from the west, large parts of the world are turning to coal. Nothing can stop this. A turn to nuclear power as rapidly as possible, supplimented ultimately by breeding, is the best long term hope.

The western obsession with a false climate crisis is certainly what Lindzen has called the greatest example of mass delusion in world history. It is doing enormous harm to states like California and Texas, and countries like Germany and England, and threatens to harm many, many more. It would be still worse if the climate industrial complex succeeds in convincing the less developed parts of world to follow its dictates. The number of premature deaths in that case, would be difficult to estimate, but would be enormous. One wonders if Abraham Lincoln was wrong in saying "You can't fool all of the people all of the time".

As we have seen, the cost estimates for the transition to wind and solar energy, made by its *supporters* runs into as much as $275T by mid century (the skeptics would say it is impossible or much more expensive). Waste of this magnitude is sufficient to ruin a civilization. All this is to take down a power system which basically works, and replace it with one which barely works only when the sun shines or the wind blows. In other words, we will be spending these hundreds of trillions to build *half* a power infrastructure. This cannot help but remind one of a similar disaster nearly a century ago. Faced with a hostile, powerful neighbor, France spent tremendous effort and treasure to build up an enormous white elephant in steel and concrete, *half* a wall. The comparison is apt.

While the harm the climate mass delusion is potentially doing to the fusion project, of course pales by comparison, it is still important. It makes fusion snake oil salesmen promise a fast solution to the non existent climate crisis. They promise something they should know fully well that they cannot deliver. When their Ponzi schemes all collapse, who knows what the harm will be to the fusion project; a project that has a real possibility of becoming one of very few possible routes to sustainable, economic and enviromentally viable energy for world civilization.

To achieve economic power by magnetic pure fusion energy (MFE), once ITER is successful, one has to proceed to the next step, the DEMO as the ITER web site says. To proceed via inertial (i.e. laser) fusion energy (IFE), there is less information on a plan to do so, but Steven Bodner, former head to the NRL program suggested a 3 step process. These last steps for each path would be very large steps, most likely taking decades, and costing tens of billions, assuming they can be accomplished at all.

This paper asserts that with fusion breeding instead of pure fusion, one can skip the DEMO if one goes via the MFE route, and can skip Bodner's final stage if one goes the IFE route. One could go from the end of the preceding step directly to commercial power. Perhaps, finally (!), fusion power really could be achievable in 35 years; and not available in 35 years as it always will be.

Fusion, and especially fusion breeding research are extremely important for the maintenance of civilization. It is one of a very small number of options for sufficient power for a future world of 10 billion people. It will not be achieved quickly, no matter how much it claims to be a quick solution to a nonexistent 'climate emergency'. There is no way to avoid the reality that either fusion breeding, and especially pure fusion, will become available only with a huge effort which will take several decades and will cost billions. But it is more than worth the investment. The continuation of modern civilization could well depend on its success.

DISCLAIMER

The products used for this research are
commonly and predominantly used products
in this area of research. There is absolutely
no conflict of interest between the author and/or
the publisher, and the products or producers thereof,
because neither the author nor publisher intend
to use this this book as an avenue for any commercial
purposes or any litigation, but only for the advancement   of
knowledge.   The knowledge the author attempts to advance are

1. The necessity for a large worldwide increase of energy for the purpose of advancing the benefits of civilization to the entire human family.
2. The fact that there is neither a climate crisis, nor a possibility of wind and solar being able to support modern civilization with at the quantity, reliability, and price necessary.
3. The fact that fusion breeding is a short cut to economic fusion, pure fusion can only come much, much later, assuming it is possible at all.

As this book is open access, anyone can use any part of this book for any purpose, as long as the material is properly cited.

Also, the research was not funded by
any producing company, rather it was funded by
personal efforts of the author.

COMPETING INTERESTS

Author declares that no competing interests
exist.

www.ingramcontent.com/pod-product-compliance
Lightning Source LLC
Chambersburg PA
CBHW050439280326
41932CB00013BA/2180